Intellec

FINANCIAL TIMES

Prentice Hall

In an increasingly competitive world, it is quality
of thinking that gives an edge – an idea that opens new
doors, a technique that solves a problem, or an insight
that simply helps make sense of it all.

We work with leading authors in the fields of
management and finance to bring cutting-edge thinking
and best learning practice to a global market.

Under a range of leading imprints, including
Financial Times Prentice Hall, we create world-class
print publications and electronic products giving readers
knowledge and understanding which can then be
applied, whether studying or at work.

To find out more about our business and professional
products, you can visit us at www.business-minds.com

For other Pearson Education publications, visit
www.pearsoned-ema.com

Pearson
Education

Executive
Briefings
@ www.briefingzone.com

Intellectual Capital

Measuring and enhancing the true value of your business

DINA GRAY

FINANCIAL TIMES
Prentice Hall

An imprint of Pearson Education

London ■ New York ■ San Francisco ■ Toronto ■ Sydney ■ Tokyo ■ Singapore
Hong Kong ■ Cape Town ■ Madrid ■ Paris ■ Milan ■ Munich ■ Amsterdam

PEARSON EDUCATION LIMITED

Head Office:
Edinburgh Gate
Harlow CM20 2JE
Tel: +44 (0)1279 623623
Fax: +44 (0)1279 431059

London Office:
128 Long Acre
London WC2E 9AN
Tel: +44 (0)20 7447 2000
Fax: +44 (0)20 7240 5771
Website: www.briefingzone.com

First published in Great Britain in 2001

© Pearson Education Limited 2001

The right of Dina Gray to be identified as author
of this work has been asserted by her in accordance
with the Copyright, Designs and Patents Act 1988.

ISBN 0 273 65402 0

British Library Cataloguing in Publication Data
A CIP catalogue record for this book can be obtained from the British Library.

10 9 8 7 6 5 4 3 2 1

Typeset by Boyd Elliott Typesetting
Printed and bound in Great Britain

The Publishers' policy is to use paper manufactured from sustainable forests.

About the author

Dina Gray is Director of Intellectual Capital at AIT Group plc.

Dina spent the first five years of her career in the Royal Army Educational Corps teaching, consulting on and implementing computer systems throughout the British Army. On finishing her short service commission she studied for and was awarded her MSc in Computer Science from Imperial College of Science and Technology. Following her degree, Dina gained valuable experience working in commercial training roles for both SCO and Cap Gemini. In 1996 she was invited to join AIT to help the company develop its staff in order to help the business gain from the obvious potential it had in its human capital. Since that time she has taken on a wider role and in 1997 joined the Board as Director of Intellectual Capital. Dina has been instrumental in looking at how the company can work smarter and profit from utilising its Intellectual Capital to gain competitive advantage.

Dina has made numerous presentations on the culture, working practices and knowledge management techniques that have been developed within AIT. She has recently joined the Knowledge Management Steering Committee of the Chartered Institute of Personnel and Development.

AIT GROUP PLC

AIT provides e-CRM solutions for the financial services industry. AIT's e-CRM software has been designed to manage and evolve customer relationships across a wide range of financial services organisations. Operating in any sales or services environment, AIT's multi-channel solutions enable a company to maximise the effectiveness of its Internet, call centre, interactive TV, agent and mobile channels through one seamless application.

AIT was founded in 1986 in a room above Maurice the Barbers in Henley-on-Thames. The company is now publicly quoted on the London Stock Exchange, boasts a 300-strong community, occupies four state-of-the-art sites in both the UK and the US and has a market capitalisation of over £300m.

AIT has always placed an emphasis on creating a culture that makes people want to work for and with them. Initiatives aimed at enhancing the culture are readily encouraged. The main aim of AIT's culture is to foster greater communication, both within the company and with their clients, investors, suppliers and the local community.

AIT places a great deal of emphasis on the relationship with its staff, a recognition that AIT operates in an industry in which skilled and experienced staff are at a premium. In 1999 AIT won the Arthur Andersen UK Best Practices Award for Motivating and Retaining Employees.

The author may be contacted at the following address:

Dina Gray
Director of Intellectual Capital
AIT Group plc
The Smith Centre
The Fairmile
Henley-on-Thames
Oxfordshire
RG9 1AP

Tel: 01491 416653
Fax: 01491 416601
Email: dina.gray@ait.co.uk

Contents

List of figures

List of tables

Executive summary

The management of a company's Intellectual Capital is increasingly becoming a focus for many organisations. These farsighted businesses want to gain an enhanced understanding of their potential for increasing shareholder value; they wish to identify what they know and want to discover how to exploit the knowledge that they already have within their organisation.

Intellectual Capital will be important to you if you wish to create profit from what you know and what you do well. Knowledge companies such as IT companies, legal firms and consultancy firms will naturally focus on selling and profiting from what they know. However, all companies can gain value from understanding, improving and exploiting the potential of the processes and stakeholders particular to their own organisation. The improvement of company processes, in order to work smarter and more cost effectively, will inevitably come about by employees sharing knowledge about the best practice of what works well and, equally importantly, what doesn't.

Intellectual Capital measurement is now being seen as a rich source of valuable information about the potential of an organisation. Intellectual Capital statements can be used to make sense of today's balance sheet and P&L figures. In fact many of the footnotes that accompany and explain the financial statements in an annual report are really an insight into the Intellectual Capital of the company.

A report on the state of a company's Intellectual Capital would ideally assure shareholders that the organisation:

- has the ability and capabilities to achieve its stated goals;
- is robust to potential changes in the operating environment;
- has thought through how the spend on education and training programmes will enhance future shareholder value;
- has researched and evaluated how re-engineering programmes will make the organisation more efficient and consequently more profitable;
- has focused on the relationships with key customers and suppliers to ensure that maximum benefit is achieved through all partnerships;
- shares knowledge appropriately to learn from past mistakes and to improve organisational performance.

Intellectual Capital can be split into three key areas:

1 Human Capital.

2 Structural Capital.

3 Stakeholder Capital.

People make an important contribution to any business. Within many organisations the investment in Human Capital is growing year on year. This investment has become necessary due to the change in working patterns, the cost of recruitment as the workforce becomes more transitory, and as employee expectations of the organisation's investment in personal development are raised. In many new economy companies the investment in Human Capital now competes with, and often matches, the investment in traditional tangible assets. In traditional business models shareholders expect to see a return on investment in a new factory or a piece of new machinery; nowadays they are also demanding to see a return on the investment in the Human Capital of the organisation. Measuring the return on Human Capital is inherently more difficult and more open to interpretation than that for traditional business measures, but this does not mean that it should be ignored.

The advent of the Internet and other communication devices means that every company, large or small, now has the opportunity to compete in the global economy. Businesses will have to devise innovative strategies to prosper from this new, faster moving world order. Smaller, nimbler organisations are able to take advantage of a situation because they can mobilise and act quickly to solve a customer's problem. Larger, more traditional companies that are steeped in corporate processes are beginning to understand that they have to reorganise and have to learn to adapt more quickly and become more entrepreneurial. However, larger companies have the advantage that they have far deeper pools of knowledge than their newer competitors; the trick is to share this knowledge and to use it to move quickly ahead with new solutions and inventions. Capturing and collating relevant corporate knowledge, then providing processes and mechanisms to share rapidly that knowledge will become ever more important in realising and profiting from the organisation's Intellectual Capital.

Relationships with customers, suppliers and even shareholders are changing and businesses now rely on building trusting, long-term partnerships to help them gain greater market share. The establishment of stakeholder relationships throughout the organisation will help sustain loyalty and maintain revenues. Understanding your customers, knowing how best to work with them and pre-empting their future needs will increase the potential for repeat business. Working with your suppliers and helping them improve their efficiency will ultimately drive down your own costs.

A number of executives may dismiss Intellectual Capital as yet another management theory that will ultimately fade and die. However, whilst reading this text, as a business leader, you should ask yourself the following questions:

- How do we plan for the future of our organisation?
- Do we have the right resources to achieve our goals?

- Do we use these resources fully and effectively?

- We have the right number of people, but do they have the right skills and experience to help us grow our business?

- Do we know if inappropriate processes stifle our company?

- How do we know any of the above? Do we monitor and measure such things in our organisation?

Introduction

DEFINITION

Intellectual Capital: an organisation's employees using best practice processes and resources to transform organisational knowledge and external relationships into commercial value.

How to profit from what you know, whom you know, and what you do well.

DEVELOPMENT OF INTELLECTUAL CAPITAL

In the 1980s the evolution of the information age became a prominent consideration for any business wishing to steal a competitive advantage over its rivals. Personalised services to demanding customers called for greater information about the needs of these customers in order to deliver satisfaction and quality on demand. Remember that telephone banking was still a dream and high street insurance brokers were still making a comfortable living. Alongside this explosion of information exchange, traditional manufacturing and industrial sectors continued their decline. The demise of the British mining and shipbuilding industries has been well documented. At the same time we began to see the formation of new companies whose only balance sheet assets were patents and people. These nimble, entrepreneurial firms traded in what they knew. They did not manufacture goods but provided services. The term 'knowledge revolution' was coined as the most critical defining moment for the world economy since the industrial revolution. At this point many academics began to look at new ways of valuing organisations that were based on knowledge capital rather than physical capital. As the academics began their research, so the more perceptive knowledge-based companies began practically to manage their Intellectual Capital and to realise their potential by converting what they knew into commercial value.

Managing a firm's Intellectual Capital to increase value is not necessarily a new concept. For years, human resource professionals have been concerned with training and developing an organisation's people, and the more astute have implemented human resource accounting to demonstrate return on this investment. Renowned, inventive companies, such as 3M, Hewlett Packard and Xerox, to name but three, have won universal admiration for their approach to, and commercialisation of, their innovations. Pharmaceutical companies have long understood the value that can be created by codifying and patenting their research. Market researchers augment their revenue by selling databases of information that other businesses can then exploit. In the last decade the spotlight on Business Process Re-engineering raised awareness of how improved efficiency and hence greater profitability could be achieved using less resources.

The reason that the term Intellectual Capital has now become a frequently discussed concept is that all of the above approaches can be pulled together under its umbrella to demonstrate how the intangibles in a company can be measured, understood and turned into real commercial value. Intellectual Capital is used to look at the business as a whole, to improve efficiency and to release the collective brainpower.

This management briefing offers a detailed and practical approach to the management of Intellectual Capital for executives wishing to measure and enhance the true value of their business.

BASIC TERMS AND CONCEPTS

The term Intellectual Capital is clouded with confusion due to the multitude of other expressions that are used in its place. Intellectual Capital is often described as being concerned with knowledge capital, non-financial assets, hidden assets and invisible assets. The following terms are often used interchangeably:

- *Human Capital* – regularly referred to as the human assets or the human resources of a company. Describing people as assets or resources limits their measurement to the purely quantitative. In a standard annual report a business will happily state that they have x number of staff, but will not, or cannot, state what these staff are capable of achieving. Human Capital accounting widens the measurement criteria to encompass what the employees of a company know, what their skills are and what they are capable of accomplishing. Training and developing employees can then be viewed as a way of increasing the Human Capital to help achieve and realise the strategic direction of the business.

- *Structural Capital* – has numerous descriptions, all of which are only subsets of the whole. Popular terms are knowledge management, process capital, intellectual assets and intellectual property. Knowledge management is a term applied to the processes used to capture and share the information that resides within the company. Other business processes, used to help the organisation run smoothly, can be grouped under the heading of process capital. The codified knowledge or information captured through knowledge management practices is frequently described as the intellectual assets of a company. If these intellectual assets are patented or copyrighted, they then become legal tangible assets and are referred to as the intellectual property of the business.

- *Stakeholder Capital* – in some circumstances this is referred to as relationship management and focuses on the relationships that any business has and nurtures for future commercial gain. In earlier texts this was often referred to solely as Customer Capital, but as recent studies have shown, businesses of the future will need to be concerned with all stakeholders, and therefore this definition has expanded. Companies need to understand how both supplier and shareholder relationships can add value to their organisation.

It is important to realise that Intellectual Capital is all of the above. Fig. 1.1 shows each of the strands must be inter-related for a business to create maximum value from what it knows, whom it knows, and what it does well.

Fig. 1.1 Relationships between terminologies

THREE KEY AREAS OF INTELLECTUAL CAPITAL

On today's stock markets businesses are valued far higher than their book value. Share prices are indicative that a business is valued not for its historical accounts of performance and this year's dividend payment, but for its ability to generate future profits. This factor has been more than evident in the dot com world. However, this is not an exclusive phenomenon to new economy companies – all shareholders want to understand the potential the business has for growth and hence to create greater wealth. Intellectual Capital management and reporting can help shareholders understand not only the wealth but also the real health of a company. Leif Edvinsson, the first ever Director of Intellectual Capital at Skandia SKS, has developed an excellent tree analogy to explain this. The traditional annual report tells shareholders why this year's fruit is plentiful; an Intellectual Capital report tells shareholders about the health of the roots of the tree and can therefore indicate whether the tree is growing stronger and will produce more fruit in the coming years, or whether it will wither and die due to poor nourishment.

Figure 1.2 demonstrates how the three elements of Intellectual Capital can be viewed when considering future profitability.

Fig. 1.2   Three key areas of Intellectual Capital

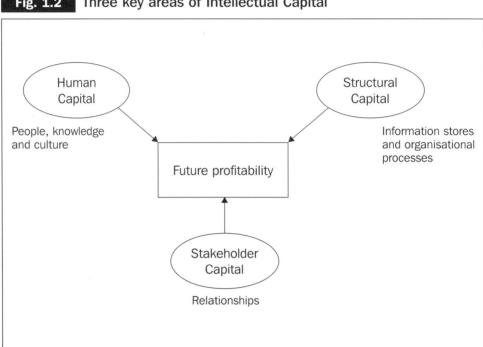

Human Capital

When deciding on the future strategic direction of the business companies need to have an in-depth understanding of the capabilities of their staff to ensure that the strategic plans can be undertaken and ultimately achieved. In order to gain this understanding an organisation needs to be able to perform a gap analysis on where the skills, competencies and abilities of the company currently are, and where they need to be in the future. Building learning and development plans to fulfil the gaps identified will ensure that the development of employees will be in line with the company's business plan and strategic direction.

Realising the return on investment when developing employees should be a strategic decision when creating recruitment and training plans. The Investor in People Standard is an excellent tool for auditing this investment. The Investor in People award has recently changed so that its indices now focus on measuring outcomes rather than processes. The award insists that all learning and development plans must be created to align with company strategy so that the Human Capital is able to fulfil the potential of the business.

Respect for the individual and the building of a strong psychological contract is essential in realising a return on the investment in a company's Human Capital. It is important to appreciate that no business owns its employees, and at the end of every day when those staff leave there is no guarantee that they will return the following morning. The incentivisation of employees to remain with a company and to share their knowledge is now an ever-increasing concern throughout every industry.

Structural Capital

The Structural Capital of an organisation is concerned with the way in which a company operates and the way in which it obtains value from what it knows and what it owns. The processes that enable an organisation to react more rapidly than its competitors and the processes that enable the organisation to function efficiently must be continually monitored and enhanced. The improvement of business processes, both operational and supportive, is an essential element of Structural Capital management.

Structural Capital is also the knowledge capital that the company owns and more importantly exploits. Once a person's knowledge is codified and written down it becomes the property of the organisation. However, only once that knowledge is used to create further products and improve efficiency will it be truly valuable.

In a study by KPMG Consulting, entitled *Knowledge Management Research Report 2000*, it was reported that those companies who had a knowledge management strategy realised significant benefits including better decision making (71%), faster response to key business issues (68%) and better customer handling (64%).

Stakeholder Capital

The Centre for Tomorrow's Company is a stalwart proponent of the theory that to be sustainable and to maintain continual competitive advantage, a company must become an inclusive company. This means that businesses need to build relationships and include all stakeholders in the strategic decisions and future direction of the company. The inclusive company sees its stakeholders as being its employees, its customers, its suppliers, the local community and its shareholders. From an Intellectual Capital management perspective the employees are covered under the previous section concerned with Human Capital. Working with both customers and suppliers in a form of partnership can enhance the relationships and increase value to all those concerned. Intellectual Capital is concerned with the management and measurement of these relationships in order to understand the benefit to the organisation.

Unipart has demonstrated that through its enhanced relationship management with suppliers it is able to drive down costs. Unipart has made substantial cost savings by helping smaller suppliers review their own processes to improve their own efficiencies so that the savings can be passed on to Unipart.

Knowing who the shareholders of the company are, and what it is they need from the company, can ensure investors maintain their investment in the company's stock.

The focus of this briefing will be to set out how a business can adapt its current organisational structure and behaviour to take maximum value from its Intellectual Capital.

2

The importance of Intellectual Capital to your business

WHY IS INTELLECTUAL CAPITAL IMPORTANT?

If you think knowledge management is expensive you should try ignorance!

Companies of twenty years ago were built to run in predictable stable economies. At the start of the new millennium we are operating in a world economy where technological advancements have become enabling factors for businesses to be able to respond more rapidly to more knowledgeable and demanding customers. This ever-changing economic landscape, where employees hold much of the power, means that businesses need to not only look at the way they operate today, but to look at their potential to operate in the near future.

Retaining knowledge

In modern society the workforce is far more transitory than at any previous time in history. Companies therefore need to be concerned about the knowledge and expertise that could walk away tomorrow. All areas of industry need to plan a strategy around the management and protection of the knowledge that is held within. Of course such a strategy can only be created if you know where specific knowledge and expertise resides. You may be thinking that this does not necessarily apply to you as you do not operate in the so-called knowledge economy. However, most companies can identify their 'gurus', those staff who have been around so long that they know exactly 'how it's done around here' and exactly where to find a particular piece of information.

Henley Regatta is a prestigious event in the English social calendar and is the oldest rowing event in the world. The various elements of the Regatta, such as marshalling, umpiring and time keeping, are each managed by long established local families. The rules and ways of working are passed down through the families by word of mouth. In addition the Regatta staff only come together for the week of the Regatta and there is very little cross sharing of localised knowledge. For the year 2000 the Regatta Office developed a knowledge management strategy in order to reduce their risk and dependency on key people.

Future potential and the creation of wealth

Intellectual Capital is a matter of creating value by applying all your intangible and tangible assets appropriately and intelligently. Understanding what you have and how it can be used can increase your ability to capitalise on the potential of your company, and understanding what you don't know can help target appropriate investment. The basis of Intellectual Capital management is about turning future earnings potential into stakeholder value noting that, for shareholders, this is usually dominated by financial capital.

The recognition of potential value has been actively demonstrated where purchasers have paid, on average, up to five times the book value for a company. If we look purely at the high technology sector and, especially in recent times, the Internet sector, then this has on occasion been over two hundred times the balance sheet value.

Book value vs. market value

The share prices of knowledge based companies have risen (and fallen) dramatically since 1999. However, in nearly all cases the market value of these companies still outweighs the total tangible assets on the balance sheet. The market makers may not describe it as such, but through their analyses of growth rate and peer group comparisons they are in fact placing a value on the Intellectual Capital of these businesses. Analysts already take into account a number of intellectual tangibles, such as patents and the value of licences. However, in the case of Internet start-up companies, we have seen the first, often not too successful, examples of the analysts valuing companies on their potential to use their Intellectual Capital for future wealth generation.

Share price is not the only area that touches on the value of the Intellectual Capital of a company. On acquisition, a business undertaking commercial due diligence will look closely at the products the target company owns and the potential of the current markets in which the company operates, will investigate its customer base and will, more importantly, look at the ability of the current management team and the skills and competencies of other valuable staff. Commercial due diligence expands the financial and legal due diligence to delve under the covers of a company to ensure that the Intellectual Capital of that company is of potential value. Properly measured and reported, the commercial due diligence procedure will build a more in-depth picture of the business being acquired.

Even if you are not running a dot com venture or pure knowledge company, or you are not intending to acquire, as you continue to read this book you should start to imagine how you could increase the perceived value of your company. What would happen if you were to publish and advertise the potential of your Intellectual Capital?

A DIFFERENT WAY OF VIEWING YOUR BUSINESS

We all know that revenue minus costs results in profit. However, many businesses have traditional views of managing budgets and looking at cost control. If you are asked to cut budgets within your company, how do you choose which budget or budgets to trim back? Can you say truthfully that you know what the impact on your business will be if you cut a particular budget? If the budget you choose to cut is the headcount budget, is your company capable of determining who are the most knowledgeable and valuable staff within your organisation?

A Board asked its senior management to look at where savings in the running of the business could be made. The senior management team undertook an analysis of the figures and discovered that the greatest spend was on telephone calls. They then sent out a directive that no telephone calls should be made before 1pm. The budget savings were quite noticeable. However, the levels of sales dropped as the sales team was now spending half of its time on the telephone to customers.

Wherever possible, from an Intellectual Capital perspective, as with R&D and marketing spend, businesses need to view their expenditure as an investment and not as a cost. As with traditional investment in physical capital, businesses should be able to demonstrate return on the investment in these less tangible elements.

Traditional accounting methods inform businesses of the value of their physical assets and the balance sheet shows a snapshot of where a business is today and not where it is going. This is a major stumbling block for companies wishing to increase shareholder value; many of today's businesses do not know if they are using the full potential of their intangible assets. Measuring and accounting for some intangibles such as Human Capital assets still does not tell companies if those assets are the correct ones for the job in hand. Viewing assets differently, measuring their current and potential value will enable businesses to distribute and fully utilise their intangible resources. What would your company balance sheet look like if you were using all of your assets to their full potential?

All companies therefore need to begin to view their businesses differently and start to measure empirically those factors that are often described as a 'gut feel'. You need to understand the areas in which to invest for the future so that you do not hamper the potential growth of your company. Simply looking at financial budgets will not tell you this; creating measurements that will better inform you will not be easy, but you should at least try.

RECRUITMENT = INVESTMENT

Recruitment of new personnel is always reported as a cost to the business. If, however, people were seen as a purchase in the same way as a piece of plant equipment, then the expenditure could be depreciated over the time that the employee stays with the company. Likewise, the additional revenue that the person is able to generate can then be seen as a return on that investment.

How intangible are intangibles?

In the newer, knowledge-based companies, the intangibles of the business are now of greater value than the tangibles on the balance sheet. However, the term 'intangible' is a little misleading. Many of the intangibles – people, systems, databases and customers – can easily be counted and even touched. Therefore do not be put off by the term intangible – in many cases these items are as tangible as the building in which you sit.

In this book you will be shown that there are a variety of opportunities and ways in which to measure your Intellectual Capital. Not only can you measure your Human Capital using traditional human resource measurement systems, but you can measure the number of databases and systems that support your business, you can measure the efficiency of your processes and you may already know the value of your trademarks, licences and patents. The secret is to pull all of these intangibles together to show their interaction and to show how the sum of the whole can enhance the true value of your business. This means creating a map or 'navigator' of your company and using it as a guide to investment decisions and the measurement of returns.

Reporting to investors

As businesses start to view themselves differently in order to understand the indicators for their future financial performance they also need to report this to their investors. Investors are poorly served by the average annual report. In its present form a balance sheet does not show the shareholder the hidden talent within an organisation. The format of most current annual reports is not conducive to showing the investor how the organisation's intangibles can turn a new entrant in the market into a major player or, conversely, show them how losing an influential senior manager could bring a loss of confidence and decrease in share price.

An investment company recently lost a highly regarded fund manager and a number of his team. The numerous letters to newspaper financial advice columns were evidence that investors were now nervous of investing in this particular fund.

Businesses need to convince others of their future earnings potential and their ability to seize an opportunity. Companies need shareholders to invest in them for their future potential, not for what they achieved last year or how much cash they have in the bank today. Businesses need to report more fully on how well they are preparing for the future, how much investment they are making in training and development, how much investment they are directing into R&D and the potential of their current markets and new products.

A DIFFERENT WAY OF MEASURING YOUR BUSINESS

The commercial world is in a state of constant change, and as the rules of the game change, so companies will have to adapt the way in which they measure and analyse their potential for fulfilling their future strategic direction. Companies are experiencing growing pressure to change their business practices in order that they can become ever more adaptive to an increasingly demanding customer base. A number of the challenges which businesses face are:

- flatter management structures;
- customer expectations of service and quality;
- the demand for more, and often sensitive, information by analysts and investors;
- rapidity of new product launches;
- frequency of partnership change and renewal;
- management techniques for dealing with:
  - a dispersed workforce
  - full-time employees becoming part-time
  - career changes
  - home working
  - virtual teams.

Examples of valid questions that should be supported by appropriate measurements:

1   Have the savings in headcount outweighed the losses in communication and knowledge?

2   Has the lack of perceived opportunity increased attrition?

3   Has the decrease in structure increased innovative ideas?

4   Has the higher level of service increased customer retention?

5   Can increased market share be attributed to the higher levels of service and quality?

6   Has investment in new products been returned within the first year?

7   Can the increased market share be attributed to the number of new products launched?

8   Is customer retention the best in the market sector?

9   Has investment in new working practices increased staff retention?

10   Is management overhead for home workers cost beneficial compared with savings in office overheads?

New measuring and accounting systems

Companies need to understand how these new challenges could impact on the value of their business, and the only way to do that is to measure and analyse the effect that these changes have on the bottom line. The impact of any change ought to be measured, and the effect of new strategies to support the business plans can then be analysed (*see* Fig. 2.1).

Fig. 2.1   Return on Intellectual Capital investment

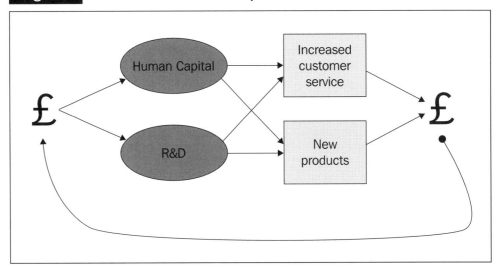

Traditional accounting measures can no longer measure the true value of what companies are worth. A retrospective look at last year's balance sheet to see how many new buildings were purchased or how the investment in machinery has depreciated is rarely effective and is subject to accounting vagaries. Even in service companies where a month by month analysis can show the revenue that was secured and the future licence fees that were sold, the accounting measures are insufficient. This analysis does not inform the executives if the company has the intellectual capability to create greater licences and increased service sales in the future, nor does it demonstrate how the investment in training and development has depreciated over the year.

The Institute of Chartered Accountants is already aware of the growing need of companies wishing to account for Intellectual Capital. In December 1999 the Institute issued a Good Practice Guideline entitled *Managing Intellectual Capital* which reported on a study commissioned by the Financial and Management Accounting Committee of the International Federation of Accountants. The conclusion of the report states that there is still a great deal of experimentation to be done before a standard approach will be considered, but that accountants have a valuable role in helping report on the wealth of measures that can be applied to Intellectual Capital.

Measuring potential

The early standards that have emerged for Intellectual Capital measurements are based around the creation of indices. Table 2.1 shows an example of a number of the different indices that have been created at AIT and a sample of the measurements used for each of these indices. Indices are a collection of measures specific to the business; they can range from direct counts (i.e. number of staff), ratios (i.e. hits per web page) or concrete financial measures (i.e. amount of revenue generated per person). Ratio measurements are useful to help determine the efficiency and productivity of a company's Intellectual Capital.

Whatever you eventually decide to measure, the measures you choose must be relevant to your own business. The measurements ought to be relatively easy to collect otherwise the discipline will be difficult to follow, and they should be kept to a minimum so that you avoid irritating staff with excessive measurement. However, these measurements also need to be accurate and worthwhile. For example, it is very easy to count the number of people in your organisation, but do you know why you are counting them?

Intellectual Capital measuring can help you review the way in which you operate. If you find that one type of capital outweighs another, for example if your Human Capital investment is high but your conversion rate into profitable Structural Capital is relatively low, you can start to investigate why. In the following chapters you will be given advice on how to devise your own indices and to look at the ratios which are important to your own company.

Table 2.1 AIT Intellectual Capital indices

Index	Example measures
Retention	Length of service Last 12 months' attrition Resignation rate Graduate attrition
Flexibility	% of home workers % of part timers % of staff on site % of contractors % of offshore developers % of staff with more than one role
Human Capital	Human investment ratio = (Revenue−total costs/compensation and benefits) Remuneration per total costs Total benefits/total compensation In-house training hours per person % industry certification External recruitment rate Acceptance rate
Structural Capital	% of static to dynamic web sites % of processes automated % usage of library books Number of white papers on the web
Efficiency	Revenue per full-time employee Outsource costs/total costs Chargeable time vs. non-chargeable time (utilisation) Average performance per person
Morale	Number of issues raised Number of issues solved Number of staff who feel valued Number of aspirations met
Culture	Number of team breaks Number of happenings (actors in the workplace) Car parking spaces per person Bikes per person Number of people in community projects
Quality of life	Excessive hours and distribution Satisfaction with family-friendly policies % of staff on official company breaks

Continued

Table 2.1 Cont.

Index	Example measures
Leadership	Number of leaders
	Ratio of leaders to followers
	Leadership training days per person
Communication	% of interaction time
	Efficiency of communication
	% of lunchtime lectures
Creativity	Number of knowledge spaces
	Amount of brainstorming floor space
	Number of new products per person

Investing for the long term

Intellectual Capital investment returns are often not immediate. A substantial investment in the development of employees or the results of a three-year research and development programme will be realised much longer term. Shareholders need to be educated that it is the investment in these intangible elements which will increase their invested capital over time and that this investment ought not to be sacrificed for short-term dividend returns. Whatever the investment in Intellectual Capital it must eventually be turned into Financial Capital. Therefore, an Intellectual Capital strategy must always be able to demonstrate how the investment will be returned through increased revenues.

3

Defining Intellectual Capital

THE NEW ECONOMY

In the agricultural revolution growing produce created wealth and a person needed to own or rent land to be able to profit. Landowners at this time therefore held the power. The Crown rewarded people for winning wars by giving them land.

As we moved on to the industrial revolution, money not land became the difference between those who were successful and those who were not. Financiers and bankers took over the landowners' power mantle. To improve and grow your business you needed money to make investments in factories and machinery. Revenue growth and wealth creation now depended on the manufacture of goods. For working in this industrial age people demanded to be rewarded with money.

Now that we have reached a knowledge revolution, intellect has replaced the importance of finance. Financial capital is not an issue; there is now a plethora of organisations willing to lend money. Revenue growth now depends on the services as well as the products that are sold. Now, more than ever, today's products are the result of the input of brainpower. Those people with intellectual capability now hold the power. The people your organisation will need in the future will be a rare and expensive commodity. The unfortunate consequence of basing your future wealth on the Human Capital in your organisation is that your employees can walk away, closing down your business, like the bank foreclosing on a loan in the industrial age. One interesting question is, does this mean that people will look to be rewarded by finding ways to enhance their personal intellectual capital? Certainly employees are now favouring those companies who are willing to invest in further training and development rather than those solely paying higher salaries.

INTELLECTUAL CAPITAL COMPONENTS

The business value of the three key areas of Intellectual Capital:

- Human Capital
- Structural Capital
- Stakeholder Capital

can be more fully understood by looking in more detail at the components of each of these areas. The components are shown in pictorial form in Fig. 3.1. Whilst this is an excellent visual aid, it is not actually possible to add Intellectual Capital to Financial Capital to get market value since they are measured in different units and are actually interwoven in complex and unique ways that vary from company to company.

Fig. 3.1 Business capital structure

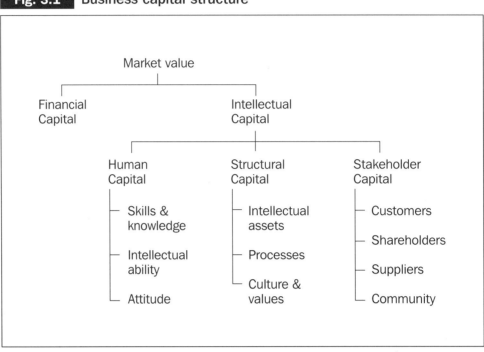

HUMAN CAPITAL

The management of the Human Capital of an organisation is concerned with the development and motivation of the employees of the company in line with the strategic direction of the business.

Skills and knowledge

The potential of the organisation to fulfil its strategic plans will depend greatly on the skills and knowledge of the workforce it employs. Many companies do not have a complete picture of the skills, knowledge and experience that their employees possess and therefore one of the first steps to managing the organisation's Intellectual Capital is to create a skills and experience map. Where there is a paucity of skills, or where there needs to be a slight change to the skills already acquired, a business will need to invest in recruitment or in training. Therefore, both recruitment and training need to be seen as an investment and not as a cost. Without the investment in acquiring the necessary skills the company will not be able to follow through its strategic plans.

Figure 3.2 is an adaptation from an illustration by Thomas Stewart in his book *Intellectual Capital, The New Wealth of Organizations** and demonstrates how

---

* Nicholas Brealey Publishing, London, 1997

the investment in Human Capital should be applied depending on the skills and the intellect of an individual. Where staff have a high intellect a business needs to ensure the provision of continual training to maintain and improve those assets. However, it is also important to recognise that some staff, however intelligent, may not be assets with their current skill sets. In this case a business needs to consider the cost benefit analysis of retraining versus releasing and replacing with more relevant staff.

Fig. 3.2   Understanding skills and ability

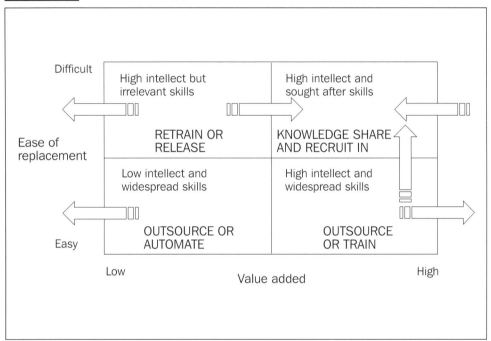

Once the required skills are in place the staff will be able to create value for the company by applying their skills to identified tasks. Ensuring that employees are given responsibilities where their skills are best utilised will give the greatest return on the investment in recruitment and training.

Intellectual ability

In the fast moving world that we are all a part of, skills learnt on one day may be out of date by the next. Different and frequently changing demands on the business means that it is necessary for employees to have the ability to adapt and apply their knowledge to solve new and challenging problems. Therefore, being able to adapt, to apply their experience in different areas and to learn new skills is an extremely important capability for all employees.

> At AIT we select new staff for their aptitude and ability to learn new computer languages and not on their knowledge of the current development environment. We extend this philosophy to our graduate selection where again we look for those who have an aptitude for computing rather than those who may have studied Computer Science for the past three years.

Investment in the improvement of intellectual ability has to be part of a much longer-term strategic plan. Increasing intellectual ability is normally achieved through traditional educational routes. Businesses can invest in the development of intellectual ability by sponsoring employees for a sabbatical to study for a post-graduate degree, or by sponsoring undergraduates through their first degree. A rarer breed of business is one which has taken a more altruistic view and financed college courses and sponsored school programmes.

However, raw intellectual ability alone will not necessarily lead to innovation and added value. It is the company's responsibility to ensure that their working practices enable the individual to be given the space, the encouragement and the opportunity to use their intellectual ability to innovate.

Attitude

Having the appropriate skills and a high level of intellectual ability does not guarantee a business that its Human Capital will return the following day. There are two aspects to retaining and motivating the staff within an organisation.

The first is to select the employees for their attitude and willingness to share what they know and apply their skills to the task at hand. All businesses need to strive to motivate their employees to give more of themselves than is being asked of them. The willingness of a member of staff to do this will depend on the psychological contract established between the company and the individual. If an individual feels valued and trusted he or she will be more willing to share what they know with the organisation and their colleagues. If an individual's personal values align with the company's values he or she is more likely to have a positive attitude to the task ahead. Company values will differ across all businesses; in a young vibrant company the values may well be based around optimism and willingness to turn their hand to any task, whereas in a large corporate department the values may be centred on stability and conformity to rules. Therefore all companies should ensure that the personality and psychometric tests used during selection are appropriate to the values of the organisation.

Most people want to give their best and therefore understanding where the company is heading strategically and understanding the part they are to play in helping the company achieve its goals will motivate them. Strategic briefings throughout the whole organisation can help align the efforts of all staff to where the business wishes to go.

> The most famous example of aligning staff aspirations behind a vision is the often reported example when President John F. Kennedy asked a cleaner at NASA what he was doing, the reply was 'I'm helping to put a man on the moon'.

Motivating staff to help the company move forward will depend on the leadership skills in the organisation. The development and enhancement of leadership capability is yet another factor in the development of an organisation's Human Capital.

STRUCTURAL CAPITAL

Whereas the Human Capital of an organisation has its own free will and can be categorised as the thinking side of the organisation, the Structural Capital of a business is concerned with all that the company owns. Structural Capital can be either tangible or intangible, and in the cases of culture, values and processes it is peculiar and specific to that organisation.

Intellectual assets

Intellectual assets are the tangible elements of a company's Structural Capital. All organisations have filing cabinets full of documents, have computer servers full of files, have databases full of information, have products and services to sell, and may have licences and patents from which they can extract value. Unlike Human Capital, the company owns its intellectual assets.

Some intellectual assets can be afforded legal protection so that their value is inherent to the business. When an intellectual asset is patented or copyrighted for licenced trading or given a trademark, the term intellectual property is applied.

- Patenting an intellectual asset means that a business has sole right to the product or invention and excludes others from copying and selling the same product. A business can extract value from a patent by using the patented idea for its own revenue generation or by selling licences to others to manufacture the product.

- Copyrighting is normally afforded to works which are written down and which contain the application of knowledge, for example literary works or computer programs. Value can be extracted from copyrights by selling the copyright itself, or allowing others distribution or licensing rights.

- Trademarks are either associated with a company or a product. A trademark can normally increase the value of a brand and will therefore often increase in value over time.

Intellectual property must be properly audited so that a business can understand what it owns and what it can extract value from. In large pharmaceutical companies patent management can often be a full-time role. Whatever the nature of the business all companies should maintain an intellectual asset register. Intellectual Capital management can then use the intellectual asset register to demonstrate and realise the value from those assets.

Processes

The processes that a company employs to conduct its business are usually specific and of value to that organisation only. One part of Intellectual Capital management is the concern with process review and the sharing and promotion of best practice throughout the organisation. Processes can be categorised into those that are concerned with quality and those that are concerned with efficiency. Processes exist to control the flow of information around a business, and the larger the business the greater the need for process management.

Whatever processes you have within your organisation, they ought only to exist to aid your business and not to hamper it. Processes need to be reviewed on a regular basis so that the business is continually striving for improvement in both quality and efficiency. One of the building blocks of knowledge management is concerned with the identification of processes to help an organisation learn from its mistakes and to share best practice.

The learning organisation

A learning organisation should not be thought of as one that allows individuals the time and budget to train. A learning organisation is one where the company, as a collective of individuals, learns from its successes and mistakes. Process review and a study of best practice can help make any business a true learning organisation.

If you think about your own business you should be able to quickly identify numerous processes. You may have a methodology to maintain the quality of product creation and you will almost certainly have HR processes for recruiting and managing your employees. But do you have processes for sharing knowledge? Do you identify best practice and have processes to share this best practice throughout your organisation? Can you produce a list of company processes and show when and how they were last reviewed? Have you ever attempted to manage the processes within your organisation? If you can say yes to the majority of these questions then you are already managing one aspect of your Intellectual Capital.

Culture and values

The principles and the ideals on which a company is founded, and then operates from, form the cultural environment unique to that business. The relationship between an organisation and its employees is based on the trust between the two parties, and this can only be developed if the values of the individual align with the values of the company. The building of the Structural Capital of a company depends heavily on two elements of a corporate culture, the cooperation and communication between individuals and groups.

Research has shown that a common trait among sustainable companies who lead their market sector is a strong cult-like culture. Therefore a well-recognised culture is a valuable asset and one that ought to be nurtured, sustained and, if possible, measured.

STAKEHOLDER CAPITAL

Stakeholders in a company can add an extra dimension to your business, they can often offer skills that you may not have, they can bring in fresh ideas to your company, and in a number of cases you may be able to share the costs of a major investment. Building strong relationships with all stakeholders can only help in building your identity and reputation in the marketplace.

As staff are treated separately under Human Capital, the four components of Stakeholder Capital are:

■ customers

■ suppliers

■ shareholders

■ community.

Each of the four components of Stakeholder Capital can be viewed similarly. Stakeholder Capital is about building relationships with each of the partners and capitalising on those relationships to the best advantage for all concerned. Unfortunately, as with all relationships, they take time to build and have to be based on a level of mutual trust. Maintaining and managing relationships is far more cost effective than forging new ones and the return on these investments can be substantial.

Customers

The manner in which you build up your customer relationships will differ depending on the business you are in. However, understanding your customers, managing their expectations and having a thorough understanding of the reasons why they have bought from you, or have moved to a competitor, is worth measuring and tracking whatever the nature of your business.

Suppliers

Suppliers should be viewed as another business that is helping you to satisfy your own customers. Where you have decided to outsource a whole section of your company it becomes essential that you work with the supplier so that there is mutual understanding of your needs. Building the relationship and helping your suppliers deliver a better service to you is becoming common practice in large companies. If the supplier is much smaller than yourself and you are able to offer training places to the supplier this could in the long term offer benefits of service.

However, this book is about managing your Intellectual Capital, and giving help to a supplier must be based on what the return on that investment will be. Where a partnership with a supplier allows you to attack a joint market the supplier relationship could grow to that of a strong alliance or a joint venture. It is normally only at this stage that most businesses will start to carry out commercial planning to manage the relationship.

Shareholders

Maintaining good relationships with shareholders and major investors can help sustain the company in the long term. The better the relationship and the trust between an organisation and its shareholders will mean that the major decisions a company needs to take will be better supported and understood. This could manifest itself through support for the reinvestment of profits, backing for a merger or acquisition, or a request for an increase in share option allocations.

Community

Building and managing your relationship with the local community may be fairly low on your Intellectual Capital priority list. However, the local schools contain your employees of the future and therefore nurturing this relationship could pay dividends in the long term. Community work is also an excellent way of developing the capabilities of your staff through 'mentoring' schemes, through the giving of presentations and through taking on responsibilities they may not have the opportunity to take within the business.

Building trust with the local community and giving them a pride in your business achievements will, hopefully, enhance your brand and may open up a whole new pool of potential employees.

INITIAL AUDIT OF YOUR CURRENT STATE

Remember that the management of a company's Intellectual Capital is not necessarily a new idea and you will probably already have a strong HR department and processes, customer focus programmes and even community and knowledge management programmes in place. This book has been written to help you identify how you can measure and manage all aspects of your less tangible assets, not just individual items, so that you can present a total picture. So how far are you from really focusing on managing and measuring your company's Intellectual Capital? You are invited to answer true or false to the questions in Table 3.1 to determine your current state.

Table 3.1 Intellectual Capital audit questions

Human Capital

1. In my company every new member of staff is selected for their attitude as well as their intellectual ability.
2. In my company every member of staff has a regularly reviewed career plan.
3. In my company every member of staff knows the company's objectives.
4. In my company every member of staff knows how they contribute to the company's goals.
5. In my company we know the skills and ability of every member of staff.
6. In my company we try to give everybody the right job so that they have the opportunity to enhance their experience and skills.
7. In my company we ensure the learning and development programmes are aligned with the company's goals.
8. In my company we measure the outcomes of every learning and development programme.
9. In my company we measure the strength of our leadership.

Structural Capital

10. In my company we evaluate our return on investment on R&D.
11. In my company we share know-how on a regular basis using a defined communication strategy.
12. In my company we have an intellectual property strategy.
13. In my company we audit all our licensing deals.
14. In my company we now the value of our brands and actively measure them.
15. In my company we know that our business processes are efficient and effective.
16. In my company there is an infrastructure to help staff fulfil their potential.
17. In my company there are mechanisms to share best practice.
18. In my company there is an infrastructure to look after the welfare of the individual.
19. In my company there are mechanisms to capture all communication and to ensure that no issues are lost.
20. In my company our corporate culture is one of our most important assets.

Continued

Table 3.1 Cont.

Stakeholder Capital

21. In my company we know who our repeat customers are.
22. In my company we evaluate the return on investment for each of our distribution channels.
23. In my company we know the personal preferences of each of our customers.
24. In my company we measure the strength of the relationships with each of our stakeholders.
25. In my company we generate new knowledge and learning by working closely with all of our stakeholders.
26. In my company we know the aspirations of each of our major investors.
27. In my company we have community programme with well defined goals and measures.

The rest of this book will now look at each of these components in more detail and give you more concrete examples of how to measure and realise the potential return on investment in your Intellectual Capital.

4

Human Capital

HUMAN CAPITAL VALUE

Although there is much rhetoric in businesses about how 'people are our most valuable assets', it is questionable as to how many companies really understand what this means for their own organisation. Just because a company spends a large proportion of its budget on training or prides itself in keeping staff happy does not mean that it understands how its employees actually add value to the business. Unless a company can necessarily show a direct correlation between the investment in its Human Capital and an increase in the creation of structural and financial capital it cannot truly understand the value its human assets contribute. As the business world moves deeper into the knowledge economy people will become a rare commodity and the investment in them will become one of the largest expenses on the balance sheet, even though no company will ever actually own these assets. Therefore understanding how your staff create financial value will be essential for directing future investment.

Valuing staff as assets

To determine the value of any asset you need to create a measurement system. However, what will this system measure? A simple starting point is to create a structure that can identify individual capabilities such as their relevant knowledge, skills and experience. Over time, this system can be extended to measure your staff's leadership potential, their managerial capability and maybe even their innovative and creative abilities. Remember that the reason you are creating this measuring system is to determine the potential for your organisation to create future wealth.

The first step is to create an asset index so that you are aware of how valuable your staff are today and which can then be used to analyse the change in value to these assets over time.

> At AIT we have devised an experience and skills development system which rates people's knowledge and skills against predetermined levels. A calculation is then performed which takes into account a person's development level, the value of their role to the business, and their length of service at AIT. Summing the individual calculations for all staff eventually gives us a value for our Human Capital asset index. Each year we are then able to review the investment we have made by comparing the difference between this and the previous year's number.
>
> *Note*: On its own a number, such as 12.16 means absolutely nothing. It is only through the comparison and the understanding of what this number means to the company that any meaningful conclusion can be extracted.

Increasing the potential value of your Human Capital can be attained in two ways: the first is through recruiting more staff and the second is to develop your current employees whilst keeping them challenged and motivated. Any measurement system that you devise should ideally be dynamic in that it is able to demonstrate that the more you develop your people, the more valuable they become to your business through their ability to move the company towards its strategic goals. It is therefore essential that when looking at increasing the value of your Human Capital, either through recruitment or through development, that you align your staff recruitment and development plans with your business strategy. In addition, tracking the investment in recruitment and training ought to be shown as an investment and then depreciated over time. The investment in training will depreciate as the knowledge and skills become lost or obsolete – in some industries this could be a number of years, in others a matter of months. The analysis of investment and the calculation of depreciation are both areas where the traditional skills of the finance team can be used to help Intellectual Capital measurements.

Understanding what value your people add and how that value is translated into financial capital will enable you to recognise what policies and processes you need to coordinate and to concentrate your effort on.

CREATING, USING AND INCREASING HUMAN CAPITAL

Traditional tangible assets can be viewed in two ways: one is their physical value and the other is the financial value that the physical assets can help create. For example, a machine not only has a resale value, but also has value in how many products that one particular machine can produce. The initial purchase costs of the machine are depreciated over time and the maintenance costs are monitored to ensure the benefits produced remain profitable. Likewise Human Capital assets can be valued not only on their cost to employ and maintain but also on their deployment in the creation of financial value. The first step for any company is to understand its investment in, and the maintenance costs of, its Human Capital. The second step is to understand how to transfer the skills and knowledge of its staff into competitiveness and wealth for the organisation.

Traditional HR practices

Human Resource management practices have in the past been focused on process. Most companies can show you their staff handbook that has policies and practices for every element of people and organisational interaction. In fact, legislation demands that many of these practices are in place.

To their credit, scores of HR departments have created HR measurements that have enabled them to benchmark their results against other companies and therefore show the commercial side of the business some tangible results for their activity. In many cases these measurements have been those easiest to collect such as headcount, absenteeism or attrition rates. More strategically minded HR managers have produced measurements to show revenue per employee, or training budget spent per employee. However, HR professionals have rarely measured business outcomes from their investment and activity and have therefore been unable to demonstrate the true value of the people to the organisation.

Traditional HR practices and measurements have struggled to help inform the business of its potential given the skills and experience that reside in the organisation.

> The Chartered Institute of Personnel and Development has advocated for a long time that people practices can enhance the performance of a business and has recently sponsored a number of research programmes to substantiate their claims. However, as they state in their 1999 briefing paper *The Impact of People Management Practices on Business Performance: A Literature Review*, they have found it difficult to persuade CEOs of this benefit without hard tangible results around value creation and return on investment. To compound the problem, the briefing paper also points out that they have also not been able to provide HR managers with any appropriate tools and methodologies to aid progression in this area.

Human Capital valuation as opposed to HR measurement and practices is about building indices for measuring employee contribution to the bottom line and enabling businesses to look at their staff from a more external perspective than the traditional internal view.

Investing in a new asset

As the world becomes ever more fluid and businesses face new challenges and need new skills, it is essential that investment is made in people who can adapt and change. All companies ought to recruit people who identify and align with the values of the company and who have the capability of carrying out a variety of roles over time. Tomorrow's company will need to be flexible and the investment in people who are willing to support this flexibility will be of paramount importance. A business will need to provide learning and development opportunities to enable people to change roles, and therefore an essential competency in today's knowledge economy is the ability of the individual to assimilate new information and then use it appropriately. Selection techniques ought therefore to be adapted to measure and inform on these aspects. There are numerous psychometric tests on the market and you should identify the ones that align with your own values and principles.

For sustainability a business needs to view recruitment as a way of increasing its Human Capital and balance this against the pragmatism needed to fulfil today's vacancy. If Human Capital is of value to the organisation then recruitment needs to be seen as a long-term investment and not as a short-term cost. Wherever possible, businesses need to think about the longer-term potential of a new recruit and not just his or her current skills, but his or her ability, attitude and cultural fit. (It is noted that having the luxury of time to recruit the ideal person or to be able to choose from a large pool of candidates is rarely the norm.) However, as Fig. 4.1 demonstrates, this is only for those categories where new recruits will add value and where they would be difficult to replace. Where employees add little value, i.e. do not have a direct impact on financial value, and have easily replaceable skills, then you should view these staff as on short-term contract to the business or outsource the work to a partner supplier.

Fig. 4.1　Investment or outsource costs

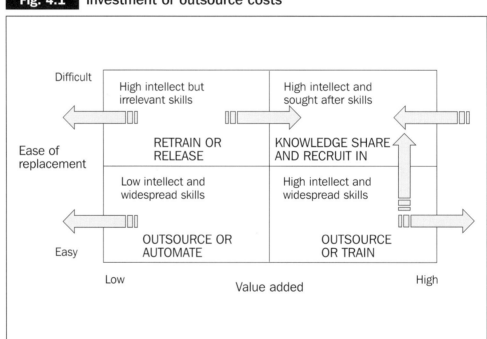

The financial investment in the recruitment of new Human Capital can return immediate value if you are able to recruit staff who possess knowledge that does not already reside in the organisation. You ought therefore to develop processes whereby your organisation can learn from your new recruit; mechanisms for achieving this immediate return are discussed in Chapter 5, 'Structural Capital'.

Measuring the return on your investment in a new Human Capital asset can be tracked through your Human Capital index and also by depreciating the expenditure over the lifetime of the asset.

Learning and development

Recruiting flexible staff into your company is strategically sound given that you allow those employees to grow and flex with your business. As with physical assets, if you do not maintain your Human Capital assets their value will depreciate. To overcome this decline in value, Human Capital assets need to be constantly developed. Developing your people does not only maintain their initial value to your organisation but can also increase that value. In Fig. 4.1 it is, hopefully, apparent that through training and development a business can enhance the value of the employees to the organisation by training them in relevant and hard to replace skills. All businesses therefore need to provide relevant learning and development opportunities to enable their people to take on new and more challenging roles.

However, having a large training budget does not necessarily enable an organisation to obtain return on the apparent investment in learning and development initiatives. Many organisations recruit a person into a role, spend vast amounts on training, and then do not review the new skills, capabilities and interests that the person has developed since joining the company. Unless your organisation understands and utilises these new skill sets you will not be obtaining maximum value from your investments in the Human Capital of your business. It would be useful for you to reflect on:

- How will you determine the skills and experience you need to meet your business goals?

- Will your learning and development strategy deliver the necessary skill changes?

- How does your organisation currently recognise and reward changes in skills and experience?

Measuring the skill base of a company is not necessarily an easy task. For many businesses the measurement will depend on the skills and knowledge involved. One frequently used measure is to track formal qualifications, both educational and vocational. However, this is not useful if roles are always shifting and the qualifications bear no resemblance to the task at hand. For example, how many of you reading this text actually call upon the knowledge accumulated in your degree course?

In order to measure the return on investment from the training budget the learning and development strategy has to support and align with the measurable objectives of the long-term business strategy. There are two processes that you may find useful to firstly plan, and secondly audit the success of the your development programmes.

- The Balanced Scorecard is a useful strategic process and tool that can be used to help determine the training needs of a business.

- The Investors In People Standard is best employed to help a company to measure the outcomes of its learning and development investment. The Investor In People Standard has recently changed from a process centric standard to one that is purely concerned with outcomes.

Both of these tools will be covered in more detail in the measurements section of this chapter.

As well as the pure cost of the training provided all organisations ought to track the cost of the time lost to the business whilst staff are developing their skills. However, an important point to remember is that your investment does not have to be in pure classroom, tutor-led training. Although it is far more difficult to track utilisation and therefore to measure the return on investment, your employees need to be given the space and encouraged to manage their own learning. Other forms of learning opportunities you could consider are:

- quiet, self-contained learning stations;
- freely available books and magazines;
- Internet access;
- computer-based training;
- subscriptions to professional societies;
- apprenticeships;
- rotation of staff through different areas of the business.

Utilisation of Human Capital assets

Investing in the right people with the most appropriate skills is only the first step in obtaining maximum value from the Human Capital of an organisation. Utilising the skills and knowledge of the staff to ensure maximum financial return is the next stage in the process. Building a skills index is a necessary step to enable an organisation to determine who has the most appropriate skills and experience for a particular task. A skills index can be simply built as a database of people with the skills that the organisation considers to be relevant and useful. The skills index can also be extended to capture the aptitude and ability of a person as well as their base skills and knowledge. Before creating the skills index you will need to carefully consider how you will:

- Capture and maintain the information. (This can be achieved through career assessment processes, performance appraisals or even through a series of testing.)
- Store and access the information. (Choosing an appropriate and easy to administer system is essential and there is a plethora of these on the market.)

To ensure that the sum of the parts of a team is greater than the whole, an understanding of the personalities, as well as the skills, of the individuals involved is also necessary. A number of well-tried and tested psychometric tools, such as Myers Briggs, can be used to determine the best team dynamics. The results of these tests can then be stored on the skills index to enable more effective use of your Human Capital assets.

To make individuals and teams work well it is also necessary to understand how they think. Many instances where teams or even whole companies fail to perform can be traced to differences in how people think and like to behave between one part and another. For example, an area dominated by well-oiled teams finds it hard to interact with groups of individualists. Understanding this and learning how to deal with it is the field of practical epistemology and there are some works on the subject such as that of Klein, Roos and Von Krogh.*

Determining the most appropriate utilisation from a central unit will not enable organisations necessarily to be flexible. Both the staff of an organisation and the business itself need to be able to respond to market needs and new commercial challenges. Therefore you ought to look at how you could encourage your staff to be proactive in recognising the skills that will be needed in the future and giving them the opportunity to identify their learning requirements. By sharing the corporate plan and the future staffing needs employees will be able to make informed decisions on the way in which they plan their development.

Emotional intelligence

Developing and measuring the value of Human Capital is about people, what skills they possess, what they know and how they behave. The latter of these competencies is the most difficult one to measure, although it is one of the most important in looking at maintaining your business culture and developing your business leaders of the future.

In the past couple of years the concept of Emotional Intelligence (EQ) has been touted as equal to, or even more important than, IQ in the success of business leaders. EQ covers such areas as:

- self-awareness
- self-motivation
- ability to deal with other people
- ability to manage and motivate other people.

Understanding the potential in your organisation for providing future leaders is obviously an important measure to add to your Human Capital index.

---

* Klein, A., Roos, B. and Von Krogh, C. (1988) *Knowing in Firms*, Sage.

Professor Victor Dulewicz and Dr Malcolm Higgs at Henley Management College have been researching the area of Emotional Intelligence and are refining their study by analysing the skippers and crews taking part in the BT Global Challenge, a round-the-world yacht race. ASE, a psychometric test company, based in Windsor, Berkshire, have worked with Dulewicz and Higgs to produce a commercial psychometric test to determine a person's EQ.

MEASURING HUMAN CAPITAL

Measuring the value of your Human Capital potential is just one element of measuring and managing the whole of your Intellectual Capital. An employee will be of value to you if they have hard to replace skills, in-depth company knowledge, an appropriate behavioural attitude and are willing to develop themselves. Determining who in the organisation has these characteristics will not be an easy or trivial task.

To value your Human Capital and to assess its potential to increase financial returns you may find the following steps helpful to follow:

- determine the skills and capabilities that your Human Capital assets will need to help you fulfil your long-term business strategy;
- using gap analysis, or Fig. 4.1, determine the need for recruitment and development;
- calculate the investment that will be needed;
- devise a measurement system to track return on investment;
- devise a measurement system to track progress against strategy.

An AIT example

On completing a gap analysis on the skills needed for the coming year, it became apparent that an increase in the number of experienced people at the senior levels within our project development teams was required. This increase in experience was necessary to fulfil our strategic plans.

Recruitment and training strategies were created to increase technical expertise and leadership skills for project team staff. At the end of the year all staff will be reassessed against well-defined competency-based development levels. In this way we will be able to demonstrate whether our investment has enabled us to increase the capability of our staff for the potential of creating future revenues.

Human Capital value is one of the most difficult aspects of Intellectual Capital to measure, and therefore any system you create ought to be well thought through and well designed. You must consider carefully what you are measuring and how these measures will establish the true potential of your business.

Return on investment

There is no doubt that for most organisations the investment in people is now a large percentage of the overall capital expenditure for the business. It is therefore imperative that a company is able to demonstrate that it is deriving maximum benefit from the investment in the recruitment and development of its employees.

To determine the return on your investment you will need to decide what areas of your company performance your staff directly affects. For example, the rate of your employee productivity may well have a direct correlation to the overall profitability of your business. Another direct business performance indicator may be to measure an individual's contribution in providing customer service and satisfaction. A number of organisations now have a customer satisfaction rating which is a contributory factor in determining an individual's performance bonus as a percentage of the overall company performance. Whatever you decide are useful indicators for the performance of your own particular business you must ensure that you understand the factors that affect the indicators in relation to your Human Capital. The measurements associated with these indicators must be relatively simple to collect otherwise the cost of the measurement exercise may outweigh the benefits of the analysis.

A word of warning is necessary at this stage. The design and substantiation of a useful system of metrics will not be a quick process. Practicality has shown that you need to devise a whole mass of indicators, measure for at least six months, revise to see if the measurements are showing any worthwhile trends, revise and repeat the cycle every six months. Table 4.1 shows a subset of the list of AIT Human Capital indicators pertinent to our own business. When analysing the results, no one section can really be used in isolation – it is the practice of viewing them all together that unleashes the power of understanding.

Table 4.1 AIT Human Capital index – a subset

Indices	Example measures
Personnel	Remuneration/revenue
	Remuneration/total costs
	Average remuneration
	Total benefits/total compensation
	Performance bonus per employee
Recruitment	Cost per hire
	External recruitment rate

Continued

Table 4.1 Cont.

Indices	Example measures
	External addition rate
	External replacement rate
	Time to accept
	Acceptance rate
	% of people returning
	% of staff used to interview
	Internal interview hours
	Cost of internal interviewing
	Total interview hours
	Number of recruits at level 0
	Number of recruits at level 1
	Number of recruits at level 2
	Number of recruits at level 3
	Number of recruits at level 4
Learning and development	Training cost per Full-Time Employee (FTE)
	Training costs/total compensation
	Training costs per hour
	In-house training cost per FTE
	In-house, external supplier cost per FTE
	External training cost per FTE
	Training hours per FTE
	In-house training hours per FTE
	External training hours per FTE
	Technical training hours per FTE
	Developmental training hours per FTE
	FTEs per Training and Development FTE
	Technical course excellents
	Developmental course excellents
	Performance of trainer (from delegate critiques)
	% industry certification
	% of feedback events per conference
	No. of web developers Level 4 – Expert
	No. of web developers Level 3 – Proficient
	No. of web developers Level 2 – Familiar
	No. of web developers Level 1 – Aware
Staff and skills mix	Number of staff at level 0
	Number of staff at level 1
	Number of staff at level 2
	Number of staff at level 3
	Number of staff at level 4
	Number of staff in x role at level 0
	Number of staff in x role at level 1
	Number of staff in x role at level 2
	Number of staff in x role at level 3
	Number of staff in x role at level 4
	(x is repeated for all roles in the company)
	Average age in the company
	% of staff with more than one role
	% of chargeable to non-chargeable
	Management FTEs/total FTEs

Hopefully you will find the measurements shown in the table helpful in aiding your understanding of what is meant by a Human Capital index. You may also find the table a useful starting point for the initial design of your own index.

As there is no international accounting standard for the Human Capital of a business it allows you to be creative and experimental in devising your own unique system. Whatever system you design you need to keep in mind that it is there to enable you to understand the underlying potential of your organisation. Therefore, be true to what and why you are measuring particular aspects. As there is no call on you to publish these figures do not get into the habit of manipulating the figures to give a positive outlook. As a Board you need to agree on the metrics you will collect and how these key performance indicators will be used to determine the health of the company and its potential to take on new challenges.

Measurement tools

There are a number of tools and methodologies that you can use to help determine the learning and development needs of your staff and to help measure and understand the return on investment in your Human Capital.

The Balanced Scorecard (Fig. 4.2), initially devised as the *Tableau de Bord* in France in the 1950s but developed and popularised by Dr David Norton and Professor Robert Kaplan, is a framework that enables the linking of objectives, initiatives and measures to an organisation's strategy. The scorecard provides a complete view of an organisation's potential and looks at the financial performance, customer perspectives, internal business processes and organisational growth, learning and development needs. The Balanced Scorecard can also be used to determine the learning and development needs of employees in support of individual business initiatives.

Fig. 4.2 Balanced Scorecard (a)

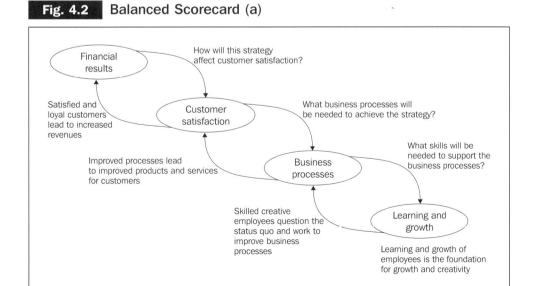

There are many companies that offer consultancy and training in the Balanced Scorecard approach. A quick search on the Internet will furnish you with a plethora of names of such organisations.

Auditing and measuring the processes and outcomes of your investment in Human Capital can be achieved through the Investor In People Standard. Investors In People is a nationally recognised standard and is competently supported through a UK-wide delivery system of Training and Enterprise Councils (to become Learning and Skills Councils from April 2000) Chambers of Commerce and Business Links. If you are interested in pursuing the standard then any of these local organisations will be able to offer you consultancy to establish where your company currently stands against each of the indicators and they will also be able to advise you on how to improve those areas where weaknesses have been identified.

The standard has recently undergone a radical change in thought. Originally it was a very process-driven standard, which meant that if you had the right pieces of paper and ran appropriate training courses you were awarded the stamp of approval. However, since 1999, on feedback from the participating recognised companies the standard has moved to one that is far more concerned with the outcomes of those processes. This is far more aligned with a Human Capital measurement perspective. Therefore setting out to attain the Investors In People Standard could enable your company to recognise its return on its investment in developing its employees.

Table 4.2 is an overview of the indicators that must be satisfied before being recognised as an Investor In People.

Table 4.2 Investor In People indicators*

Commitment

An Investor In People is fully committed to developing its people to achieve its aims and objectives.

1 The organisation is committed to supporting the development of its people.
2 People are encouraged to improve their own and other people's performance.
3 People believe their contribution to the organisation is recognised.
4 The organisation is committed to ensuring equality of opportunity in the development of its people.

Planning

An Investor In People is clear about its aims and its objectives and what its people need to do to achieve them.

5 The organisation has a plan with clear aims and objectives which are understood by everyone.
6 The development of people is in line with the organisation's aims and objectives.

Continued

Table 4.2 Cont.

7 People understand how they contribute to achieving the organisation's aims and objectives.

Action

An Investor In People develops its people effectively in order to improve its performance.

8 Managers are effective in supporting the development of people.

9 People learn and develop effectively.

Evaluation

An Investor In People understands the impact of its investment in people on its performance.

10 The development of people improves the performance of the organisation, teams and individuals.

11 People understand the impact of the development of people on the performance of the organisation, teams and individuals.

12 The organisation gets better at developing its people.

* © Investors In People

To help with the creation of Human Capital indices it would be beneficial for you to look at the work carried out in the field of human asset management. EP-Saratoga Europe is part of an international group of companies that has developed standard measures for human asset measurement, benchmarking and best practice. Saratoga produce an annual Human Asset Effectiveness Report which, in the first instance, can give an idea of what measurements may be useful for your own business, and secondly, enables you to benchmark your results against other companies. One useful feature of the Saratoga report is that it discusses what the measurement may be able to tell you about your business. Below is an example of a Saratoga benchmark and a typical description for the use of the measurement:

$$\text{Revenue per Full-Time Employee (FTE)} = \frac{\text{Total sales and service Revenue}}{\text{Total FTEs}}$$

Revenue per FTE by itself only provides an indication of how much money employees are either directly or indirectly bringing into the business. Comparatively low revenue per employee may indicate that higher emphasis needs to be placed upon marketing and sales efforts, potentially requiring redrawing of structures, changed competencies, or refocused remuneration systems. However, it must be combined with a series of other metrics to draw any firmer conclusions.

Continued

Two main factors influence this benchmark: revenue and employment levels. People interventions have a significant influence on both these factors. For example:

- Training, compensation and staffing issues can affect outputs, quality and sales–people interventions can therefore clearly impact revenue.

- Restructuring, downsizing and recruitment can have a dramatic effect on Revenue per FTE – these actions can of course positively affect the ratio, but by itself do little to improve the success of the organisation.

Ultimately the measure of Revenue per FTE can be a reflection of whether the organisation's people policies are having a positive effect on money coming into the business.

EP-Saratoga Europe can be contacted by email on saratogaeurope@epcg.com or through their website at http://www.epcg.com.

To help measure the costs of recruiting, compensating and training employees you could use Human Resource Accounting techniques. Applying a Human Resource Accounting system to your business may enable you to increase the accuracy in your decisions for Human Capital investment and return.

Eric Flamholtz, in his book *Human Resource Accounting – Advances in Concepts, Methods and Applications*,* discusses the concepts around Human Resource Accounting and gives some in-depth practical examples of how to account for and therefore measure the return on the investment in your Human Capital for management and financial reporting purposes.

PRACTICAL APPROACHES

Things to do and check

The following list assumes that you are starting with a blank page, obviously this will not be the case. You may like to use the following as a checklist for your future actions.

Short-term tasks

- Research the most appropriate Human Capital planning, measurement and auditing tools for your organisation.

---

* Kluwer, Hingham, MA, 1999

- From the long-term business strategy define the skills and core competencies needed now and in the future.
- Build competency frameworks that include learning and attitudinal behaviours.
- Measure the EQ of your staff.
- Build a skills and experience map of the company.
- Build a skills and experience database.
- Understand how your people think.
- Carry out a gap analysis between the current skills and experience map and the future skills and experience needed.
- Devise a Human Capital skills index appropriate to your business.
- Create a recruitment and training strategy based on the gap analysis.
- Research the most appropriate Human Capital recruitment selection techniques and tests.
- Research the most appropriate Human Capital measurement tools for your Intellectual Capital strategy.
- Create a Human Capital measurement index as part of your overall Intellectual Capital index.
- Make the growing of Human Capital a high priority in the budgeting process.

Longer-term strategic plans

- Create a positive attitude to sharing knowledge and learning.
- Create a rewards structure to positively encourage the behaviours you need.
- Develop retention strategies for high value staff.
- Devise an auditing and reporting mechanism for the return on investment in Human Capital.
- Create a leadership development programme to match your culture and business needs.
- Build and maintain a learning culture.

Structural Capital

STRUCTURAL CAPITAL VALUE

An organisation's Human Capital will develop products and patents, create and follow best practice procedures and create and evolve the corporate culture. It is this continual formation and renewal of a company's Structural Capital that gives an organisation its indefinable strength. Focusing on and improving the way in which business is conducted and the organisation is structured will eventually enable a company to improve its operating efficiency for increased financial return.

The evolution of a company's Structural Capital is best viewed as strata of process and corporate knowledge being built up over time, in tandem with and to support the development of the business (*see* Fig. 5.1). Small businesses will only have a very thin layer of Structural Capital, but as these businesses grow they will need to develop more structure to support their changes in growth and direction. An organisation with fewer than 80 employees can often function with little Structural Capital due to the fact that employees all work in close proximity to each other, knowledge is easily shared and everyone's contribution can be instantly recognised. As a company grows it undoubtedly reaches a size where staff become geographically split, effortless knowledge sharing becomes more difficult and the fairness of recognition and reward becomes an issue. At this point the organisation will need to formalise a small number of processes to replace the former natural interaction and informal recognition of individual contributions.

Fig. 5.1 Structural Capital layers

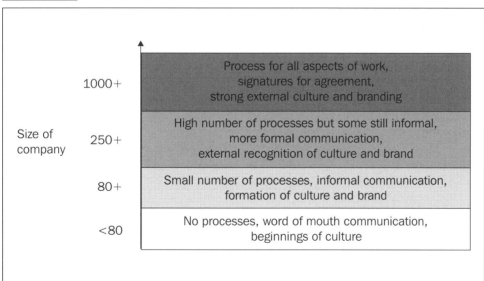

The building of Structural Capital is a way of capitalising on the investment in the knowhow of the organisation. The Structural Capital of an organisation can have value in its own right or it can be valued on its potential to facilitate the creation of revenue. The value of an organisation's Structural Capital can only truly be realised when the more intangible assets help create real financial returns.

Structural Capital has two distinct elements:

- tangible intellectual assets such as products, patents and trademarks;
- intangible assets such as methodologies, knowledge and cultural philosophies.

Intellectual assets are the more tangible elements that can be sold and for which a direct return on investment can be realised. To capitalise the value of the more intangible elements of an organisation's Structural Capital a business needs to be able to understand and measure the longer-term benefits of the investment in changes to infrastructure. Gaining a competitive advantage by improving efficiency through the application of new business processes ought to be carefully designed and then measured.

There are strong inter-connections between all aspects of Intellectual Capital management. The Structural Capital of an organisation is built and sustained by the Human Capital of the business. Structural Capital elements such as cultural influences, leadership and management philosophies will help motivate and therefore retain the Human Capital of the organisation. Structural Capital value is therefore hard to measure in isolation from Human Capital as both influence the outcomes of each other.

INTELLECTUAL ASSETS

Valuing the intellectual assets of a business is one of the easier aspects of Intellectual Capital management. Intellectual assets, such as patents, products and brands, tend to be the more tangible of the Intellectual Capital intangibles. For many of you reading this text you will probably already know the return on the investment in your intellectual assets, but do you really know if you are obtaining the maximum value possible and can you truly predict their future value?

Products

Measuring the return on the investment in a product line ought to be part of all good business practice. Undoubtedly your current product investment measurements take into consideration:

- the cost of the original research and development for the product;
- manufacturing infrastructure cost;
- marketing and cost of sale;
- cost of support for the product.

Modern business practices have concentrated on maximising the return on existing products and, of course, traditional financial measurement systems are geared to report on this form of revenue stream. However, if your business measures purely show the return on old products, investors will begin to worry about the potential for future growth (*see* Fig. 5.2).

Fig. 5.2 Product values

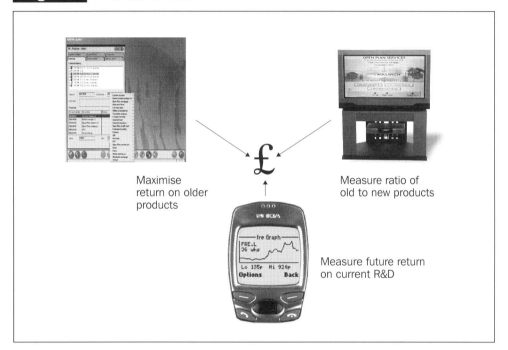

Maximise return on older products

Measure ratio of old to new products

Measure future return on current R&D

At this point it is useful to note that Intellectual Capital management and measurement is not about looking backwards but is there to help you realise your sustainability in the future marketplace. It is therefore essential that businesses are able to predict the return on investment for any new research and development programme by creating a measurement system that takes into account the life expectancy of the new product with respect to the total cost and effort for its development. When designing your Structural Capital measurement system you may find it beneficial to take into consideration the ratio of revenue from new to old products.

If you are now measuring new product investment it is only a small step to consider how you could report on this investment and predicted returns to your investors. An Intellectual Capital report is an ideal way to do this.

Patents and copyrights

In addition to products your business may also own a variety of patents. A patent is a property right that does not allow other people to copy and sell your intellectual inventions. However, a patent will only be of value to your business if you have actually utilised and exploited it. The pharmaceutical industry is one sector that has recognised the need for patent portfolio management and can demonstrate a substantial value increase through this form of management.

> The Dow Chemical Company is a large player in the pharmaceutical industry.
>   Over the past 6 years Dow has undertaken a number of projects to manage and extract value from its patents. The first of these projects was to audit and classify all of its patents. This project enabled Dow to reduce its patent tax maintenance by $40 million over the life of the portfolio. In another project Dow identified all of the key patents throughout its businesses and was able to increase its annual income through patent licensing from $25 million to $125 million a year over this six-year period.

Extracting value from intellectual assets can therefore be as simple as managing and understanding the assets you already have within your business. A starting point could be to ask yourself these simple questions:

- Do you know exactly what patents you have registered?

- Do you know the value that your patents have returned within their lifetime?

- Do you know the value that your patents have returned over the past year?

- Does the cost of protecting the patent outweigh the value it returns to the business?

- Do you know the cost to the business of the unused patents your company owns?

In some industries copyright is the strongest legal form of protection that can be applied to intellectual assets. Pure financial return on licence agreements is an easy aspect to measure and account for. However, as with products and patents, just because the measurements demonstrate the existence of a revenue stream they do not show if the maximum return is being achieved. Managing licence agreements and policing the agreement to ensure that copyright is not being infringed could increase the value of your intellectual assets through very little additional effort.

Brands

In the 21st century the brand of a product or service, and hence the company is an essential element in the customer's decision to buy. Measuring and managing the value of your brand is not a simple project and can become a full-time role. Constantly monitoring the brand and identifying ways in which it can be strengthened have become essential elements of some Intellectual Capital management strategies.

Marks & Spencer have been a well-known high street store for many years. The brand has always been synonymous with the purchase of good quality clothing basics, such as underwear, shirts and jumpers, for reasonable prices. However, as new designer labels have become more affordable, the M&S brand has suffered and the downturn in business has been greatly publicised. Interestingly, the Marks & Spencer reputation for food staples is still strong and upholds the original quality image associated with the brand.

ORGANISATIONAL STRUCTURE AND PROCESSES

To gain competitive advantage through the exploitation of organisational structure and business processes, companies must take time to reflect on, and if necessary improve, the ways in which they operate. Corporate culture, company structure and business processes are those elements of Structural Capital that are difficult for competitors to emulate wholly. Many organisations will have similar ways of operating, but it is the combination of all of these elements that makes companies individualistic in their performance.

As it is the sum of the whole and not individual components that give a company its unique operating prowess, it actually calls into question the value of benchmarking one company's processes against another. Looking at a subset of a company's processes and not understanding the causal affects of other Intellectual Capital components may give false readings and may lead to erroneous conclusions and harmful changes to your own business.

A firm recognised that its attrition rate was higher than the industry average. Sensibly they incentivised all senior managers, with the promise of a new car, if they were able to cut their divisional attrition rates by 3%. As would be expected, the managers worked hard on this target, only to be disappointed by no new gleaming top of the range automobile. In the final analysis it was discovered that no savings had been made because the recruitment team had not been told of this new target and had spent the whole recruitment budget recruiting the initial targeted headcount.

As a competitive business you should be striving to set your own standards and incorporating best practice learning from a variety of sources. Your success will hinge on your ability to design the practices to increase organisational efficiency and your managerial capability to successfully implement these practices.

Best practice

The identification of internal best practice and the monitoring of industrial best practice ought to be a high priority for all organisations. Gaining competitive advantage simply by working smarter is an attractive and obtainable goal.

> A semi-conductor company generated $1.5bn in annual free wafer capacity by transferring best practices amongst its 13 fabrication plants.

Best practice encompasses not only those processes that enable you to improve the productivity and quality of your outputs but also those processes that enable your organisation to function more efficiently and therefore cost effectively. There are four basic stages in obtaining maximum value through best practice:

- define
- experiment
- reflect
- improve.

As a business becomes established and business processes become better defined, so these stages need to be raised into the consciousness of the organisation so that continual process improvement becomes a business process in its own right.

Process control to increase productivity has been the primary focus for businesses throughout the industrial age. Successful businesses will have already identified the processes that enable them to produce their products faster than their competitors, and no doubt these processes are constantly monitored and measured. However, these processes and their measures will only ensure survival and not growth.

In the knowledge age, businesses need to build internal processes that can amplify the speed of knowledge transfer throughout the organisation and therefore improve the efficiency in those working practices that are proven to create value. Improving knowledge processes will enable a company to build upon its learning and knowledge stores and therefore facilitate the future growth of the business (*see* Fig. 5.3). In defining knowledge transfer practices for your own organisation it would be beneficial to look not only at the formal processes in place but also to try to identify the informal processes. It is usually these informal processes which if removed would have a detrimental affect on your business.

The processes that support the day to day general running of your business also need careful monitoring to ensure that they are enabling rather than hampering your operation. Your Human Capital is an expensive commodity and you should not, therefore, restrain its productivity with inefficient and clumsy administrative processes. Considering how to automate those internal processes that are manpower intensive so that your highly valued Human Capital can be freed to realise its full potential could be a financially rewarding project.

Fig. 5.3 Best practice

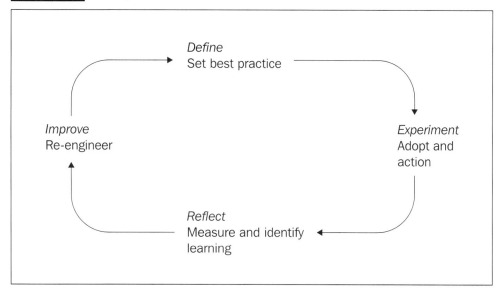

Define
Set best practice

Experiment
Adopt and
action

Improve
Re-engineer

Reflect
Measure and identify
learning

Cisco Systems is an $18bn company and has been growing by 50–60% a year. Cisco currently has over 35 000 employees and has achieved efficiency through administering its world-wide workforce through an automated technology system.

To ensure that best practice is continually identified and adopted an organisation needs to review how it is structured and understand how, or if, it rewards and encourages the sharing of best practice. Managers must be seen to openly support best practice and ensure the right people are in place to implement it.

At AIT, Vocational Groups are collections of professional staff who have a common role within the organisation. For example, one vocational group is concerned with the testing of the software. The Vocational Group heads are set objectives to identify and enhance best practice within their vocations and between themselves and other vocations. The achievement of meeting these objectives is rewarded through the annual bonus scheme.

Over the past twenty years quality management practices have been improved through internationally recognised standards such as ISO9000 and globally publicised procedures such as Total Quality Management. Although your business may already employ a Quality Manager, or indeed dedicate a whole division to quality monitoring and improvement, have you ever considered consolidating the management and measurement of these practices under the umbrella of Intellectual Capital? The efficiency and quality practices of your business are essential elements of your Structural Capital.

KNOWLEDGE MANAGEMENT

Organisational knowledge encompasses elements of information, experience and insight. Company information is wholly owned by a business and the challenge is to identify, capture and share that information widely throughout the corporation to improve operating efficiency and to facilitate organisational learning. Knowledge is largely held by individuals and is only available to an organisation to the extent that effective processes are put in place to develop and share that knowledge and freedom and space is given to individuals to use their judgement and interpretation to apply that knowledge appropriately. Organisations learn by sharing information freely, and effective organisational learning is dependent upon the appropriate combination of people, culture, technology and working practices.

The vast majority of academic writing in the arena of knowledge management has concentrated on the definition of knowledge terminology and complex theoretical models rather than on practical examples that would enable companies to realise true business benefits.

To be pragmatic, the theory can be distilled into two basic definitions:

- Explicit knowledge is information that can be documented. Explicit knowledge is found in company handbooks, on web pages, in proposals, in instruction manuals and in company databases.
- Implicit knowledge is what people know but can't necessarily write down. Implicit knowledge is the accumulation of learning and the application of that learning to solve complex problems.

Your organisation will probably already have a considerable amount of explicit knowledge; however, it is the organisation, collation and accessibility of this knowledge that is paramount to its successful exploitation.

> Over the past five years some of the large consulting firms have pursued an explicit knowledge strategy storing and sharing items such as proposals, guidelines, benchmarks, market analyses and presentations. Their recent dramatic increase in revenues has been partially attributed to this level of knowledge re-use.

As companies grow and become more geographically dispersed it is imperative that all corners of the organisation understand what explicit knowledge already exists and how it can be accessed. One obvious benefit of explicit knowledge management is that it enables employees to quickly find an answer to a problem that has already been solved in another area of the organisation.

> Whilst travelling in a taxi, from Newcastle airport to Peterlee, I was able to observe a practical application of explicit knowledge sharing. As we approached a junction it was apparent that the traffic was particularly heavy. Immediately the driver contacted his colleagues to inform them of the congestion. In return he was told of other routes that were running freely and we reached our destination on time. Customer satisfaction was rewarded with the immediate return of a larger than normal tip.

Managing the knowledge within your company will enable you not only to gain increased value from the existing knowledge but also to create new learning and knowledge in the process. Within knowledge intensive organisations the speed at which explicit knowledge is transferred, internalised and implicitly applied becomes an important factor in gaining that crucial competitive advantage. Employees need to be encouraged to share implicit knowledge in an environment of trust and mutual recognition. The value to your business will be truly recognised when your employees are able to increase their implicit knowledge and apply this learning for the good of your company.

Organisational learning

The learning organisation is an organisation skilled at creating, acquiring and sharing knowledge, and at modifying its behaviour to reflect new knowledge insights. The creation of an organisational learning policy is an essential component of any knowledge management strategy. Organisational learning is both an outcome and a process and not only encompasses the identification and adoption of best practice but more importantly concentrates on how to re-implement success and how to learn from mistakes so that an organisation can continually renew itself.

Companies that are able to identify why they have been successful and can learn from what has failed in the past will naturally increase the value of their Structural Capital. However, you cannot leave to chance the fact that organisational learning will take place – you have to create and manage the process that will help facilitate the capture of the learning and then make possible the sharing and carrying forward of that learning. Any organisational learning process should capture the key elements of the experiences of individuals and teams and then proactively transfer those experiences to the larger organisation.

A Learning History is a technique whereby you can facilitate story-telling around the successes and the challenges of a particular piece of work. During personal interviews an experienced facilitator will allow individuals to recount their stories and seek to uncover hidden learning points. Once all the individual accounts have been collected they are then aggregated to produce an overall theme for a combined story illustrated with anecdotal evidence.

The skilled facilitator can then use the story with the next group who will be undertaking a similar assignment. The story is told to the learning group and they are asked to identify what they would have done differently given the same situation. To ensure that learning has taken place teams can then set themselves identifiable learning points and record the actions they undertook on encountering similar challenges. These records will be useful as this team will also create a learning history at the end of their project.

Over time a company will own a collection of these stories which when read together will create an organisational learning history.

Measuring the learning that has taken place and therefore the return on the investment in the time spent reflecting is essential. As with the example of the Learning Histories, knowing what you have learnt and why can be added into the overall knowledge schema of your company.

A knowledge methodology

The substantial investment in increasing the knowledge and ability of employees is particularly risky when you consider that those employees could leave your organisation at any point in time. Early proponents of knowledge management insisted that companies could protect their investment by capturing all the implicit knowledge and making it explicit. Those companies that wanted to mitigate the risk in their investment in Human Capital then spent many hours and thousands of pounds developing systems to capture, collate and share this information. It soon became apparent that the writing down of all that people knew was not only difficult to determine but took an inordinate amount of time to do, and what is more, within a short space of time that information became obsolete. Motivating people to go through this exercise once, maybe even twice, was reasonably difficult, but after that became virtually impossible. If after reading this briefing you decide to instigate a knowledge management initiative *do not under any circumstances* attempt to codify implicit knowledge.

As knowledge management theory has progressed so the studies and theoretical models have evolved. However, academics have not particularly helped those in business as the models have been highly complex and the books describing the theories have been substantial tomes.

What has become apparent is that a knowledge management strategy needs a simple methodology to follow in order that a process can be developed and measurements duly applied to identify business success. Figure 5.4 shows the methodology that has been devised and adopted at AIT. It is not based on any one theory but helps us understand where we are with specific knowledge initiatives.

Fig. 5.4 **AIT's knowledge methodology**

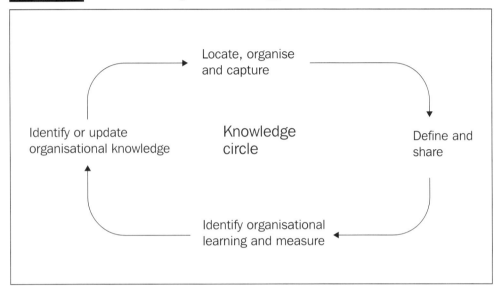

The knowledge topology of your organisation will be in a constant state of flux as your organisation evolves and learns, and therefore the employment of a full-time Knowledge Manager is a must.

Identifying organisational knowledge

To create an understanding of and to identify the explicit knowledge or information needed to enable your organisation to function effectively, and to identify who may hold implicit knowledge that they would be willing to share, you need to create two knowledge maps. A knowledge map helps identify:

- what you already know;
- where that knowledge is;
- what you need to know.

An explicit knowledge map identifies where in the organisation information resides, who is responsible for its creation, and who needs to know that the information exists.

ASLIB – The Association for Information Management is a charity registered in 1924 whose 2000 members are private and public sector companies and organisations throughout the world, concerned with managing information resources efficiently. The skill of developing a knowledge inventory often falls to those with librarianship skills. ASLIB run courses and offer consultancy on knowledge mapping. More information on their services can be found at http://www.aslib.co.uk.

The explicit knowledge identified in such a map can cover processes, documentation on past learning, past proposals, past presentations and past learning histories. Table 5.1 shows an example of an explicit knowledge map. How the information is categorised and sorted will be dependent on your own organisational needs.

Table 5.1 Explicit knowledge map

Type	Information	Location	Who needs to know
Presentation	Corporate	c:\sales\pres\corp.ppt	Whole company
Document	Bid template	Filing cabinet in sales office, and r:\sales\templates\bid.doc	All sales people All senior project managers Senior finance managers Resource manager
Web page	Share price	http://coweb/finance/share	Whole company All investors
Process	New starter	Does not exist	Facilities manager Support manager Finance manager

An implicit knowledge map is an extension to the skills and experience database built to track your Human Capital investment. It is the Human Capital of an organisation that owns the implicit knowledge and therefore you need a map of who has what experience and what particular projects or aspects of work they have participated in. The two pieces of additional information that need to be added to your skills and experience database to transform it into an implicit knowledge map are where a person resides in the organisation and how they can be contacted. The goal of the implicit knowledge map is to put people in contact with each other.

Locating, organising and capturing

The knowledge maps provide an ongoing and current view of the state of your knowledge assets. They can be used to highlight the potential gaps that represent areas of risk, vulnerability or ineffectiveness, thereby providing the focus for and input into the following stage in the methodology. This step in the methodology is to locate the existing knowledge, organise it and create the knowledge that has been highlighted as deficient.

A knowledge item may already be located and appropriately organised but not captured in such a way as to be easily accessible to those people who need it. One of the roles of the Knowledge Manager is therefore to decide on the most appropriate storage medium commonly known as a knowledge repository. A knowledge repository is something in which knowledge can be stored and could cover any of the following:

- files, in 'old-fashioned' filing cabinets
- electronic documents
- work folders
- databases
- spreadsheets
- web pages
- personal organisers
- videos
- training material
- books and magazines
- individuals' heads.

The Knowledge Manager has a responsibility to ensure that the knowledge repositories are current, relevant and easily accessible by those who need to store or update information (*see* Fig. 5.5). The maintenance of knowledge repositories can be time-consuming and therefore the aim should be to create simple, easy to follow storage processes. Having an understanding of how the knowledge will be shared ought to enable a better design of the repositories.

The most difficult aspect of this phase of the methodology is knowing what you don't know. Being able to identify what knowledge is incomplete needs either an in-depth understanding of the organisation or a network of people throughout the organisation who are able to help identify the missing components. Once the knowledge gaps have been established the Knowledge Manager will need to decide how to create or bring in the required knowledge. Depending on the nature of the knowledge needed it could be recruited in, it could be the purchase of a marketing database, it may be the creation of a process or methodology or it may be to develop the organisation's people.

Fig. 5.5   Role of the Knowledge Manager

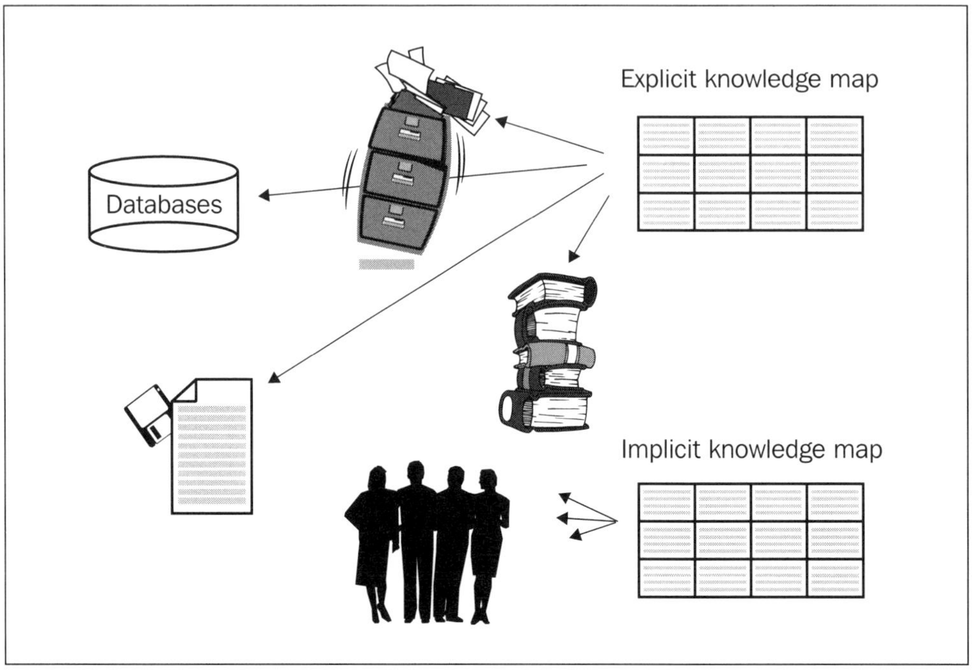

Defining knowledge elements

Experience has shown that it is extremely useful to define attributes for each individual knowledge item within the explicit knowledge map. An attribute can be simply thought of as a label that tells you specific information about that knowledge item.

An example is the attribute that defines the life span of the knowledge item. The 'Time to Live' attribute will enable the Knowledge Manager to determine the best medium in which to store it and will enable that piece of information to be purged once it has become obsolete.

Email – 'Time to Live'

For the majority of emails, their life span is dependent on the time it takes for the recipient to read the email and to decide its fate. However, if an email is sent to inform the company that someone has left their lights on, or that cakes are in reception, that email should be recalled and therefore effectively killed off once the lights are switched off or all the cakes have been eaten. Modern email systems allow you to recall or set a time attribute on your emails.

Other attributes that need to be considered, assigned and added to the knowledge map are shown in Table 5.2.

Table 5.2 Knowledge attributes

Attribute	Importance
Owner	The person responsible for keeping the information up to date. This is important to the Knowledge Manger who has to be told when to update the knowledge map or to know who to chase for latest updates.
Sharing mechanism	How should the information be shared? Should it be sent to the recipient, known as a push mechanism, or should it be placed in a convenient place to be accessed when the recipient is ready, known as a pull mechanism. The sharing mechanism is important as it enables the Knowledge Manager to determine the ideal repository and sharing technology – see below.
Relevance	Names of those who should be given access to this information. This will be important for pull type information such as web pages.
Audience	Names of those who need to be told that the information has been created or updated. This will be important for push type information such as emails.
Time to live	When will the information be out of date and how will it be disposed of? Disposal is important as it could be deleted or it could be archived.
Format	Specifies the format the information is currently in and whether it is replicated in other formats. This is important to enable the most suitable repository to be established.
Importance	If this flag is set then those receiving the information can prioritise the order in which the information is received.

Disseminating knowledge

Once collected, organised and defined the appropriate sharing mechanism can be established and adopted. Different sharing mechanisms are more appropriate than others depending on the sharing attribute. Table 5.3 shows some examples of different sharing mechanisms depending on whether the information should be pushed, allowed to be pulled, or needs to be a combination of the two.

Table 5.3	Sharing mechanisms

Push mechanisms	Pull mechanisms
Email	Newsgroups
Lectures	Intranet
Company meetings	Newsletters
Training courses	Notice boards

Push and pull mechanisms
Team meetings
Communities of practice meetings
Apprenticeships
Video conferencing
Telephone
Talking to one another

Disseminating knowledge is concerned with giving people access to solutions and to other experts within the company. Sharing explicit knowledge is a simple case of determining the most efficient way to enable the target audience to access the information. In many cases explicit knowledge is best shared through the use of technology. However, implicit knowledge needs to be shared through the basic human process of talking to one another. Finding implicit knowledge solutions is concerned with the more difficult aspect of organisational cultural change.

Sharing explicit knowledge – the power of technology

This section of the book will try to give you a flavour of the latest technologies available that can enable explicit knowledge sharing. However, let us not fall into the standard trap of assuming that all explicit knowledge needs to be shared through the use of technology. The use of libraries, training events, notice boards and company newsletters have been performing this role for many years. The issue is, of course, that the speed of knowledge dissemination through these mechanisms can be slow and cumbersome. When planning your knowledge strategy, it is necessary to decide which is the most appropriate knowledge sharing mechanism for your own organisation.

One of the most successful explicit sharing mechanisms used at AIT is *Communikhaze*. This is a weekly A4 newsletter that is posted on the back of the toilet door. It is undoubtedly the most read piece of explicit information within our hi-tech company.

In recent years there has been a proliferation of knowledge management tools (Fig. 5.6). Initially these tools tended to be database query tools just re-badged with the knowledge tag. However, more recently, a number of true knowledge tools have come to market that are based on complicated mathematical algorithms.

Fig. 5.6   **Knowledge-sharing mechanisms**

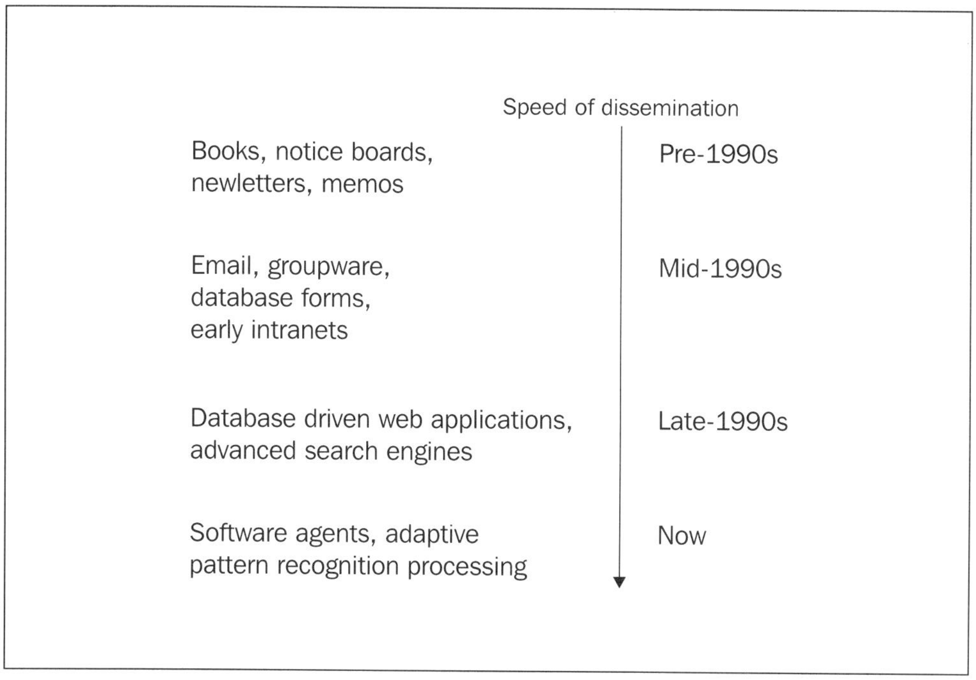

Speed of dissemination

Books, notice boards, newletters, memos	Pre-1990s
Email, groupware, database forms, early intranets	Mid-1990s
Database driven web applications, advanced search engines	Late-1990s
Software agents, adaptive pattern recognition processing	Now

Some explicit knowledge tools perform the combined role of information repository and sharing mechanism. However, if you already have a number of disparate explicit knowledge stores you will need a tool that is able to search each of the repositories, retrieve the required information and then display the results in a digestible format. Therefore, when considering a tool you should research how the technology will package the knowledge and how it will enable sharing.

There are two essential components of a knowledge-sharing tool: the first is how it searches for and retrieves the stored information; and the second, how it displays the information to the user.

Whatever software you eventually choose, it will require a powerful search engine as it will have to handle information in any format, located in any part of your business or, indeed, the world. At the heart of any successful search engine is the algorithm it uses to interrogate the specified repositories. The most recent search engines use adaptive pattern recognition algorithms that are able to analyse any piece of text and identify the context of the written word rather than the word itself.

A context-based search engine is often used in tools that employ software agent technology. Software agents can be directed to investigate specified sources of information, defined text sources, web sites, server directories and emails. The user can build a search profile and brief the agents on what to retrieve. The more advanced agent-based software can also put the user in touch with other people who are searching for the same information.

Autonomy Systems have produced an active web product that automatically examines the concepts, not keywords, in your active window and delivers links to other relevant information. The Autonomy product allows you to search the World Wide Web, the content of your company network, similar users in the Autonomy community and relevant encyclopaedia entries or books that match the subject.

Kenjin is a single-user version of Autonomy that can be downloaded from the web. If you are interested in technology then this freeware will give you a flavour of what is now possible. Kenjin can be downloaded from: http://www.kenjin.com.

As the interfaces to the available tools will differ, you will also need to consider how to obtain a consistency of approach across the whole company. Groupware tools and company intranets can often provide the solution to this dilemma.

Please do not make the mistake of basing your knowledge strategy around a particular tool. It is important that you employ only technologies that suit your company and your people and are in support of your overall knowledge aims.

On paper it is difficult to describe vividly the power of these latest innovations, so do research the wide variety of tools available and always ask to see how they have helped other companies achieve their knowledge visions. Seeing the technology in action will be far more exciting than can ever be conveyed in this book.

Sharing implicit knowledge – a teaching culture

The risk of knowledgeable staff leaving the company is a very real one in today's competitive marketplace. One way to retain valuable implicit knowledge within the business is to ensure that an individual's internalised knowledge is passed on to other people within the organisation. The aim of an implicit knowledge-sharing strategy should be to encourage people to share and disseminate their knowledge, learning and experience. Implicit knowledge-sharing can therefore be realised through the creation and encouragement of a teaching culture.

All organisations have their gurus – those employees who have a recognised in-depth specific industry or organisational knowledge. The initial step in an implicit knowledge management strategy is to identify your experts, and the second is to set in place mechanisms for disseminating the experience of these gurus.

> In ancient communities knowledge was disseminated through story telling. Elders would tell these stories whilst sitting around campfires. The folklore of how things were done was consequently passed down through the generations.

Fostering a teaching culture will take time; how much time will depend on your current company culture. The difficulty with creating a teaching culture is that many people, especially those in a culture that values personal technical expertise, see knowledge as power. The challenge is to encourage a culture that recognises individuals for their ability to coach, lecture and share their own knowledge. Intelligent people will soon realise that not only is their reputation enhanced through this change in outlook but that they are able to gain further learning for themselves which enriches their own knowledge. One method to effect this change is to set all staff individual knowledge-sharing objectives, for example to run seminars, to chair formal discussion groups or to create electronic chat rooms. The ultimate aim of an implicit knowledge management strategy is to ensure that all of your experts are coaching and passing on their wisdom and thinking.

> At AIT, an apprenticeship role, called a Director's Assistant, has been created. The DA has to work closely with the Director to gain an understanding of how they think, why they make decisions, and recognise the networks in which they operate.

Nothing is better than face to face exchange for passing on knowledge and confirming that the recipient has understood and internalised the learning. One of the objectives of an implicit knowledge management strategy ought therefore to be to facilitate ways in which people can network. Much networking and sharing happens naturally in meetings, social events and 'around the coffee pot'. Although people will meet by accident on a stairway or in the smoking room, an organisation can facilitate unplanned knowledge-sharing opportunities.

> Knowledge Spaces are designated areas, situated near coffee machines, that can be equipped with either high stools and a bar or comfortable seating and low coffee tables, a printable white board for writing down ideas and a small reference and magazine library. Knowledge Spaces are normally created to facilitate 'bumping into' each other and to give people a place to meet and share ideas.

In organisations spread across multiple sites, or multiple continents, face to face knowledge-sharing opportunities are difficult to achieve. In these situations technology can enable a teaching culture through the use of electronic discussion groups, video conferencing and web seminars.

Whatever the size or geographical dispersion of your organisation, implicit knowledge sharing can only really be achieved through the creation of a teaching culture that instils the principle of always looking to pass on the thing that you have just learnt.

Hewlett Packard has an established knowledge-sharing culture that is encouraged through their intranet, which prompts users with a pop-up menu that asks 'Should anyone else see this?'

AN ORGANISATIONAL KNOWLEDGE STRUCTURE

A knowledge management strategy can be split into three distinct stages (*see* Fig. 5.7):

■ creation of explicit and implicit knowledge maps;

■ creation and organisation of knowledge repositories;

■ creation of knowledge-sharing mechanisms.

The company's Knowledge Manager therefore needs to have a mixture of skills; he or she needs to be an organiser, cataloguer, technologist and evangelist.

Fig. 5.7 The knowledge structure

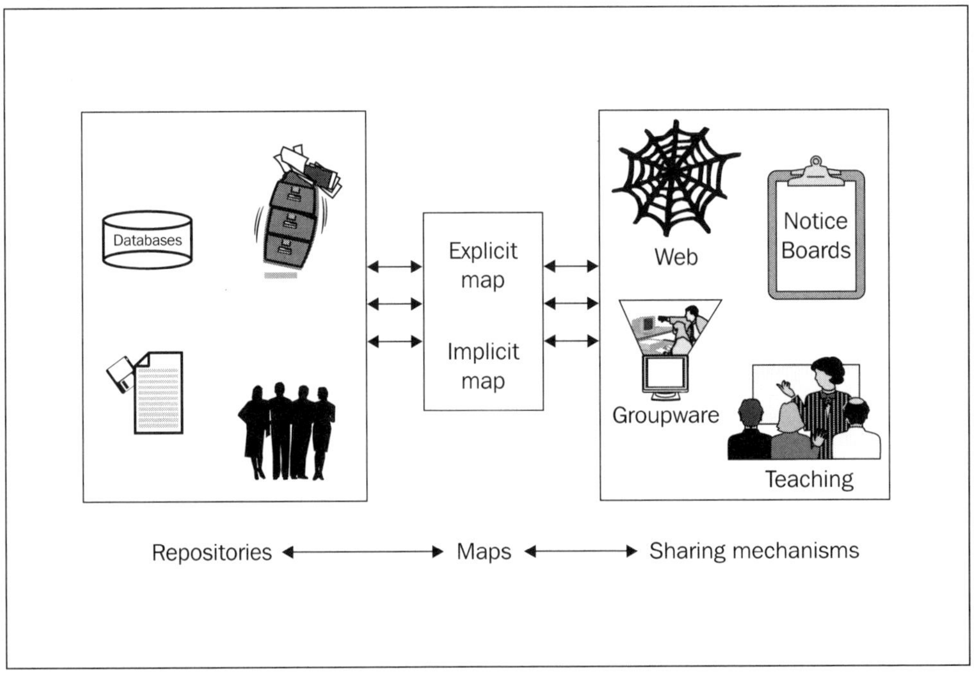

MEASURING STRUCTURAL CAPITAL

Measuring the Structural Capital of an organisation is, in some cases, a matter of measuring real financial capital return and, in others, is about measuring the return on investment in improving business practices.

Intellectual assets

Evaluating the return on intellectual asset investment is quite simply a matter of measuring the financial return from each individual asset. For example, it should be easy to track the number of new products sold versus the number of old products sold. Measuring the return on patents and licences is normally covered by existing accounting procedures.

Processes

If you are looking to improve elements of best practice you need to decide on process performance targets at the outset. As the outcome of improving best practice is hopefully to increase efficiency and productivity, your performance targets should be designed to reflect these aims.

Table 5.4 shows the initial components of an index that was created to measure the current efficiency of a business.

Table 5.4 AIT efficiency index

Index	Example measures
Efficiency	Resource gap in days
	Revenue per FTE
	Costs per FTE
	Net operating costs per FTE
	Profit per FTE
	Wealth created per FTE
	Cost of goods sold/total costs
	Outsource costs/total costs
	Total productivity
	Core productivity
	Chargeable time/non-chargeable time
	% of time on appraisals
	% of time on career development
	% of time on administration (non-admin.)
	% of time in training
	% of time in T Groups
	Average performance per person

These same measurements can then be used to track the changes in efficiency after the completion of a process improvement initiative.

Knowledge management

The first step in measuring knowledge management effectiveness is to create a Knowledge Management Index to measure tangible knowledge elements (Table 5.5).

Table 5.5 AIT knowledge index

Index	Example measures
Knowledge	% of static web sites
	% of dynamic web sites
	Usage of static sites
	Usage of dynamic sites
	Number of processes automated 100%
	Number of processes automated 50%
	Number of processes automated 25%
	Number of processes automated under 25%
	Number of books in the library
	% of usage of books
	Number of magazines subscribed to
	Cost of magazine per FTE
	Number of presentations on the web
	Number of newsgroups
	Number of white papers on the web
	Size of the production intranet
	Hits on the web per FTE
	Number of training days per FTE run by internal staff
	Number of lunch-time presentations
	Number of news groups

As with process improvement, the effectiveness of a knowledge-management initiative can be measured by tracking how the programme has affected both the efficiency and knowledge indices. You should also consider how your knowledge index indicates improvements in best practice, product re-use and stakeholder relationships.

> General Electric uses a job rotation programme to help transfer knowledge throughout the organisation. GE has reduced the delay between order and delivery by 75%, reduced inventory by $200m and increased ROI by 8.5%.

As knowledge management is a relatively new business concept you may like to evaluate how close you are to having a complete strategy. KPMG Consulting has carried out research into the current state of knowledge management within British businesses. This has culminated in them releasing a report entitled *Knowledge Management Research Report 2000*, of which a copy can be obtained from their web site at http://www.kpmg.co.uk/kpmg/uk/services/manage/pubs/km2000.pdf.

KPMG have created a Knowledge Journey benchmark that is reproduced in Table 5.6. You are invited to use this to determine how far your own organisation is along the knowledge-management path.

Table 5.6 The KPMG Consulting Knowledge Journey benchmark

Key to a KM programme are:

People

- Implementing KM training/awareness (e.g. workshops or roadshows)
- Appointing knowledge officers and creating knowledge centres
- Incentivising and rewarding knowledge working
- Building and developing 'communities of practice'
- Establishing formal KM networks (e.g. dedicated workers in discrete groups, or communities of KM practice)

Process

- Benchmarking or auditing the current situation
- Creating a KM strategy
- Implementing new systems for communities of practice
- Designing other KM processes

Content

- Creating a knowledge map
- Implementing knowledge policies
- Measuring intellectual capital

Technology

- Carrying out a knowledge system audit or assessment
- Implementing ways to share best practice
- Use of KM software (either dedicated or Intranet or Groupware software)

Where is your organisation on the **KPMG Consulting Knowledge Journey**?

Stage 1 – Knowledge chaotic: 3 or fewer of the above

Stage 2 – Knowledge aware: 4 or more, drawn from at least 2 sections

Stage 3 – Knowledge focused: 6 or more drawn from at least 3 sections

Stage 4 – Knowledge managed: more than 2 from each section

Stage 5 – Knowledge centric: all

PRACTICAL APPROACHES

Things to do and check

The short-term tasks below must be a part of your overall Structural Capital strategy and you should identify the return you wish to make from undertaking each of these tasks.

Short-term tasks

■ Build and maintain a patent asset register.

■ Draw a knowledge map and make a distinction between implicit and explicit knowledge.

■ Locate and organise all explicit knowledge.

■ Provide books and magazines and publicise their existence.

■ Appoint a Knowledge Manager.

■ Create knowledge spaces.

■ Create learning spaces.

■ Provide Internet access for all.

■ Create structures to promote face to face knowledge sharing.

■ Set up communities of practice.

■ Identify your gurus.

■ Set up apprenticeship schemes under the company gurus.

■ Identify the key obstacles to successful knowledge sharing.

■ Create an induction process that teaches best practice and emphasises the value of knowledge sharing.

Longer-term strategic plans

■ Create a knowledge vision.

■ Create a brand management programme.

■ Create a Structural Capital measurement system.

■ Build and maintain a learning organisation.

■ Build and maintain a teaching culture.

■ Develop a compensation system that rewards improvement in processes and best practice.

- Design your organisation so that knowledge sharing is facilitated and enabled.
- Work towards building a positive attitude to sharing.
- Build accountability for knowledge management into existing roles.
- Design and build a technological solution to provide knowledge on demand.

Stakeholder Capital

6

THE STAKEHOLDER MODEL

Intellectual Capital management is not solely concerned with looking internally at your staff, your processes and your products. Those external companies and individuals who interact with your company on a daily basis are not only the people who will buy your products, or invest in your company, but they are also the stakeholders who will support and work with you to achieve your corporate goals. You should therefore consider all external stakeholders as a potential source of new skills and a seam of untapped knowledge. The ability of organisations to exploit the combined knowledge of all their stakeholders will be a key factor in their ability to succeed and grow.

Investing in the maintenance of existing partnerships is far more cost effective than forever having to woo and foster new ones. Measuring the return on this investment is therefore important. Intellectual Capital management can help with the measurement of the cost of maintaining those relationships and valuing the benefits that those relationships have brought to the company. If you are incorporating external knowledge into your organisation, or sharing the use of valuable databases, then there is an obvious overlap with your Structural Capital strategy. If you are recruiting from the local community or using suppliers in an outsource capacity then there is also overlap with your Human Capital strategy. Stakeholder Capital can therefore be built into the totality of your overall Intellectual Capital management strategy.

The stakeholder model is concerned with building trust and loyalty with each of your company's stakeholders, investing in sustaining those relationships, and measuring the impact of those relationships on your business goals.

CUSTOMER CAPITAL

As competition increases market share becomes ever more crucial. Retaining current customers, increasing the customer base and selling more products to existing customers has become the aspiration of all those in the commercial world.

It has been shown that each of us owns seven financial products in our lifetime, from our bank account, to our mortgage, to a personal pension. However, we never normally have more than two of these products with any one individual company. Therefore, financial services institutions have realised that they do not necessarily have to increase their customer base; they instead have to build stronger relationships with, and sell more products to, their existing clients.

Knowing the buying patterns and needs of your customers, along with their propensity to remain loyal to your business, are both important factors in helping you understand where to target future investment. If a customer is relatively new, then figuring out the potential in growth of that customer for repeat business will be crucial. Knowing how many of your customers are repeating customers, and why, will enable you to track trends over a period of time. If a customer is well established, then knowing how much they have bought in the past and measuring their current loyalty will also be of value.

Loyalty within the last decade has been encouraged through the use of awards for frequent purchases. Supermarkets have been in a loyalty club card war, and airlines have tried to encourage preferences through the allocation of air miles that can be exchanged for free flights. However, shrewd customers now swap their loyalty depending on the rewards on offer. Businesses therefore need to reconsider how to build true customer loyalty.

Customer Capital is therefore not about defining your current market share but about looking at the strength of the relationships with current customers to increase future market share.

Customer Capital investment

Customer loyalty and individual buying patterns are not normally reported to investors; it is usually only total revenues that are traditionally accounted for. However, a company does need to understand the profile of these customers so that they can direct future investment to ensure the maintenance of key relationships.

Exploiting the potential of your market is these days not just about selling more products, but is also about how you service your customers. Understanding who your customers are, knowing what it is they wish to buy, and anticipating their future buying needs means that the talk of today is not just of customer service but of 'total personal service'. Therefore a business needs to realise what it is that keeps each of their customers happy to enable them to work out how much investment to put into each individual relationship.

A customer relationship can be enhanced if you know how frequently an individual customer wishes to be communicated with, and then you allow each customer to control the levels of contact. Appreciating the way in which your customers wish to interact with your business is ever more important, as having a choice of interaction channels has increased with recent technological advances. Customer Capital investment must now consider not only the return in attracting and maintaining customers but also the return on the investment in each of these channels to market.

Cranfield School of Management and Microsoft have recently released a report entitled *Releasing the Value of Knowledge*. This study has shown that 90% of high performing companies have identified customer satisfaction as a key performance indicator. These organisations use technology to learn more about their customers and use that knowledge to increase customer satisfaction.

The definition of Customer Relationship Management (CRM) is evolving. Originally it referred to basic customer interaction. However, newer, more sophisticated CRM technology can now analyse the customer database, predict future buying potential and then target appropriate customers with specific information.

Telephone banking has now been a reality for a number of years and those who are happy to embrace technology will already be carrying out their personal banking through the Internet, through their television or via their mobile phone.

A number of financial institutions have obviously analysed the ROI through these channels as we have recently seen a number of bank branch closures. Whether this move has harmed the overall customer relationships with these organisations remains to be seen.

The investment in attracting new customers and retaining current customers can be quickly lost if the customer-facing staff of your organisation do not fully appreciate their role in maintaining these relationships. If this is the case, you should consider directing a proportion of your Human Capital investment into the development of customer relationship skills.

Structural Capital investment, in the form of knowledge management programmes, can have a direct effect on Customer Capital returns. Building knowledge about customers' habits and needs can be realised through the use of appropriate knowledge strategies.

The KPMG study has shown that of those companies with a Knowledge Management programme, 61% could access data profiling the purchasing patterns of an individual customer and 78% could identify who had last spoken to an individual customer or why the organisation had won an account within four hours, as opposed to 38% and 64% respectively of those without a Knowledge Management programme.

Sharing knowledge and information with your customers may demonstrate to them your desire to build a longer-term relationship. The investment in knowledge-sharing technology may be expensive although the returns, through increased loyalty and the gains in your own knowledge, could outweigh the costs.

SUPPLIER CAPITAL

Many businesses rely on their suppliers to supply them in a timely manner and in a cost efficient way so that they can continue to function and build competitively priced products for their own customers.

Building trusting relationships with suppliers should mean that they will provide your business with a better service and be willing to help your business in times of unusual demands. Supplier relationships often take time to establish and investment in strengthening those relationships can be cost effective. Ideally you want your supplier to remain loyal to your business and not to disappear if another customer offers more favourable financial terms. The cost of finding a new supplier and building another relationship will often outweigh the investment in sustaining the original relationship.

Where a supplier is a service provider and you have outsourced part of your business to that supplier a greater level of collaboration will be needed and a stronger trusting relationship will need to be established.

> Due to the shortage of skilled knowledge workers in the UK software industry, there has recently been a move by a large number of companies to outsource development to suppliers in India. The difference in time zones and in cultures has demonstrated the need to build mutual trust and understanding with these suppliers.

The strongest possible supplier relationship is undoubtedly when you and a supplier identify a joint opportunity and form a strategic alliance or joint venture to attack a particular market.

Supplier Capital investment

The initial investment in Supplier Capital will be the time spent identifying the suppliers who are able to provide the products and services to your exacting requirements.

If your preferred supplier is unable to give you a competitive price because they have inefficiencies in their own organisation, you could consider helping them to improve their business processes. This investment should only be considered if the supplier's cost reductions will eventually be passed on to your own customers. As well as giving advice on best practice you could also invest in your supplier by either giving them access to your facilities or offering them the opportunity to train alongside your own staff. Developing knowledge-sharing opportunities in this way could also increase the knowledge in your own organisation.

Supplier Capital investment should therefore be used to build supplier relationships in order to help your business achieve its own strategic goals.

SHAREHOLDER CAPITAL

Allowing a business the freedom to function and to take far-reaching decisions will depend on the level of trust and understanding that a company is able to build with its major investors. Having a high turnover of investors or having shareholders that wish the Board to act in the interests of short-term gains could be detrimental to the longer-term strategic direction of the company.

An Intellectual Capital management strategy therefore needs to consider how to keep investors better informed about the long-term prospects of the company. Investors will want information that will enable them to make decisions about their future relationship with your business. The return on this investment should be realised in better market valuations and in the support the company obtains in raising financial capital.

Shareholder Capital investment

For many companies the only contact they have with their shareholders is once every year at the AGM. If, however, you wish to invest in your Shareholder Capital, you should investigate the ideal way to communicate with your investors and build an understanding of the kind of contact and information they wish to receive from the company.

Investment in Shareholder Capital is therefore concerned with communication, how often you communicate, the quality and sensitivity of the information you provide and the mechanisms you provide to enable feedback to your organisation.

COMMUNITY CAPITAL

Businesses should see themselves as having a responsibility to the communities in which they exist. The level of responsibility will differ depending on the extent of influence that a business has on the world. For smaller companies their contribution may be local, working with local schools and the local community by offering employment opportunities, or by the giving of their time to fulfil community needs. For large, multinational organisations their responsibility may extend to cover a national programme, for example working with underprivileged children, or creating a policy of employing mothers returning to the workplace. Community Capital will therefore mean different things to different companies.

> The IT industry is experiencing a chronic skills shortage which could be eased if the industry was able to attract more women. Unfortunately most female school pupils do not view the IT industry as a potential source of interesting employment.
>
> At AIT this has been tackled in two distinct ways. At the local level we work with local schools, colleges and universities to market the roles within the IT industry to all interested parties, and at a national level we work with an organisation called Women In Computing, that is attempting to persuade more women to join the industry.

Building relationships with all areas of the local community will take time. To build trust in your organisation you ought to make local contacts and invite the community into your business, as this should enable better understanding of how each of you can help the other.

The return on the investment in working with the community ought to be realised as more local people apply to become employees, as new business opportunities are identified, and as staff undertake work that helps their personal development.

Community Capital investment

Working with and supporting Community Capital is not something that can be done in an *ad hoc* way. As with all other forms of investment you should consider your objectives for working with the community and what return you expect from such an investment. Investment can be in the form of financially supporting local events or in the giving of time and effort to helping with community initiatives. Whatever form of investment you choose, the outcomes and returns must be measured.

Working with the community can give your staff developmental opportunities. Outside of the workplace employees can develop their customer relationship, facilitation and mentoring skills. For inexperienced staff, community programmes such as pupil mentoring should offer them the opportunity to gain coaching and leadership experience.

If you wish to build up local contacts you will probably find that quite a bit is already happening within your area. The government has created regional Education Business Partnerships that have measurable targets and this may be the way in which you could start to become involved. Whatever community programme you decide upon it must based within the context of what it is you are trying to achieve as a business.

MEASURING STAKEHOLDER CAPITAL

Investment in any of the Stakeholder Capital elements is essentially concerned with establishing and nurturing the relationship. You need to understand where to apply the investment and what the return on that investment is likely to be. Intellectual Capital management should enable your company to review the measurements for each stakeholder and then relate the results to areas of Human Capital and Structural Capital.

For each of the stakeholder relationships a number of the measurements can be duplicated:

- number of customers, suppliers, shareholders and community programmes;
- annual sales per customer, annual purchases per supplier, annual share purchases per investor, number of recommendations by community members;
- number of customers, suppliers, shareholders and community relationships lost;
- customer, supplier, shareholder and community visits to the company;
- days spent visiting customers, suppliers, shareholders and the community;
- staff numbers in ratio to customers, suppliers, shareholders and community involvement;
- satisfaction scores per customer, supplier and shareholder;
- expense per customer, supplier, shareholder and community member.

Customer Capital measurement

All businesses should be able to produce figures to show the number of current customers and the revenue generated by that customer base. However, Customer Capital measurement is not about raw number crunching, but is concerned with the quality of the customer relationships and the potential of those relationships to generate future business.

The creation of a Customer Capital index (Table 6.1) should therefore consider the investment directed to building those relationships and measuring the return on that investment. Although customer loyalty is reasonably intangible, it is an asset and ought therefore to be measured.

Table 6.1 Example of a Customer Capital index

Section	Example measures
Customer relationship investment	Customer contact visits per employee
	Marketing spend per customer
	Sales spend per customer
	Training spend per employee in customer skills
	IT investment for customer interaction per customer
	IT investment in distribution channels per customer
	Number of account managers per customer
Customer loyalty	Customers lost in the past year
	New customers in the past year
	Ratio of new to established customers
	Number of complaints
	% of repeat business to new business
	Customer satisfaction score
Customer return	Number of customers
	Revenue per customer
	Revenue per customer recommendations
	Ratio of leads to closed sales
	% of market share

Supplier Capital measurement

If you are investing in building long-term relationships with trusted and respected suppliers you need to ensure that the investment is providing the expected returns. Supplier Capital measurements are more difficult to put in quantifiable terms as the level of investment will differ greatly across all businesses. However, measuring the cost of services or products provided against what competitors pay, or tracking the cost of products from a particular supplier over a period of time, should be common to all.

The level of investment in your Supplier Capital will be dependent on the ability of your suppliers to add value to the offerings to your own customers.

Measuring the turnover of your suppliers may tell you more about your organisation's value as a customer than about the quality of your suppliers. If your supplier turnover rate is high you should critically review your supplier relationship management.

Another aspect of measuring the investment in your Supplier Capital could be to determine how a joint initiative has improved the results in your Customer Capital index.

Shareholder Capital measurement

A good stockbroker ought to be able to give you statistics on the turnover rate of your shareholders, how long a particular investor has held shares, and how many new investors have been attracted to the holding.

Through communication with major shareholders you could establish other measurements, such as satisfaction with the last dividend payment and the potential for growth of a particular holding.

Community Capital measurement

As your community programme becomes more sophisticated and the relationships become wider and more varied you should ensure that the investment is helping to fulfil your original objectives.

A number of companies already produce community measurements in their annual reports. Table 6.2 shows an example of a Community Capital index.

Table 6.2 Example of a Community Capital index

Section	Example measures
Community investment	Employee hours spent on community work
	Community spend per relationship
	Training spend per employee for community work
	Number of community events run
	Remuneration for community officer
	Number of teacher placements completed
	Number of work experience placements completed
Community return	Community relationships lost in the past year
	New community relationships in the past year
	Number of community relationships
	Direct recruitment through community contacts
	Number of press articles about the community programme
	Number of business leads generated by the community programme

PRACTICAL APPROACHES

Things to do and check

As with the other areas of Intellectual Capital there are a number of things that you can do to work towards a more inclusive approach.

Short-term tasks

- Establish the frequency of contact with your stakeholders.
- Ensure customer relationship skills are part of your Human Capital strategy.
- Investigate knowledge-sharing opportunities with each of your stakeholders.
- Investigate what help you could give your suppliers to drive down costs.
- Make contact with local community groups.
- Devise a community programme with measurable objectives.

Longer-term strategic plans

- Devise a system to measure stakeholder loyalty.
- Create a programme to help you understand the preferences of each of your stakeholders.

7

An Intellectual Capital strategy

AGREEMENT AND BUY IN

Fundamentally changing the way in which your company views and measures value will need agreement and support at all levels throughout your organisation.

The creation and maintenance of social structures to build Intellectual Capital represents a significant investment. Therefore all directors and senior managers need to believe that identifying and measuring your organisation's Intellectual Capital is important for the future of your business. All parties have to demonstrate the commitment that will be needed to help you rethink your organisation.

Your employees will more than likely be used to working in a traditional environment and will understand the rules and the reward systems of that structure. You may therefore have difficulty in persuading staff of the benefits of knowledge exchange. You need to encourage and reward your employees to develop themselves and to build Structural Capital. Aligning your learning and development strategies with those of the business should help your staff to understand how their personal contributions can contribute to the overall company direction.

As employees realise the benefits of knowledge sharing through smarter working, the acceptance of these new work practices should become easier. Directors and senior managers can help this adoption by acting as role models in knowledge exchange and through the encouragement of personal development.

IDENTIFICATION OF ASSETS AND MEASUREMENT

The essential element of an Intellectual Capital management strategy is the identification of the intangible assets in your company, these assets being your people, processes, products, brands, explicit and implicit knowledge, and the relationships you have with each of your stakeholders. An Intellectual Capital approach will enable you to look at these assets from a new perspective and help you to understand how the management of these intangibles can realise true business value.

Creating an accounting system for Intellectual Capital is important, but more important is the consideration of how each of the Intellectual Capital components fit together to build a balanced measurement system for the whole of your company.

Measurement systems

The most successful Intellectual Capital measurement tools are those that inter-relate each of the components to help a business understand the cause and effect between Human Capital, Structural Capital and Stakeholder Capital, and help show how each of these components singularly and collectively affect the creation of financial capital. Four such tools are:

- Lief Edvinsson's Skandia Navigator™.

- David Norton and Robert Kaplan's Balanced Scorecard.

- Intellectual Capital Services Ltd's IC-Index™.

- Intellectual Capital Services Ltd's HVA.

The first two tools represent first generation measurement in that they are best suited to the measurement and comparison of value creating potential. The IC Index™ is second generation and is a dynamic tool best suited to comprehensive but company-specific value creating assessments. The HVA is third generation and combines the best features of both earlier generations. Within the limits of this book it is not possible to go into the detail of how these models work. If you are interested in learning more about any of these models you will find that each of the architects has written a number of books that give additional implementation details.

The Skandia Navigator™ is a general model that was developed to assist Skandia to measure its Intellectual Capital (Fig. 7.1). The Skandia Navigator™ has been designed to provide a balanced picture of the company's Financial and Intellectual Capital; it concentrates on the relationships between five key areas of focus.

Fig. 7.1 Skandia Navigator™

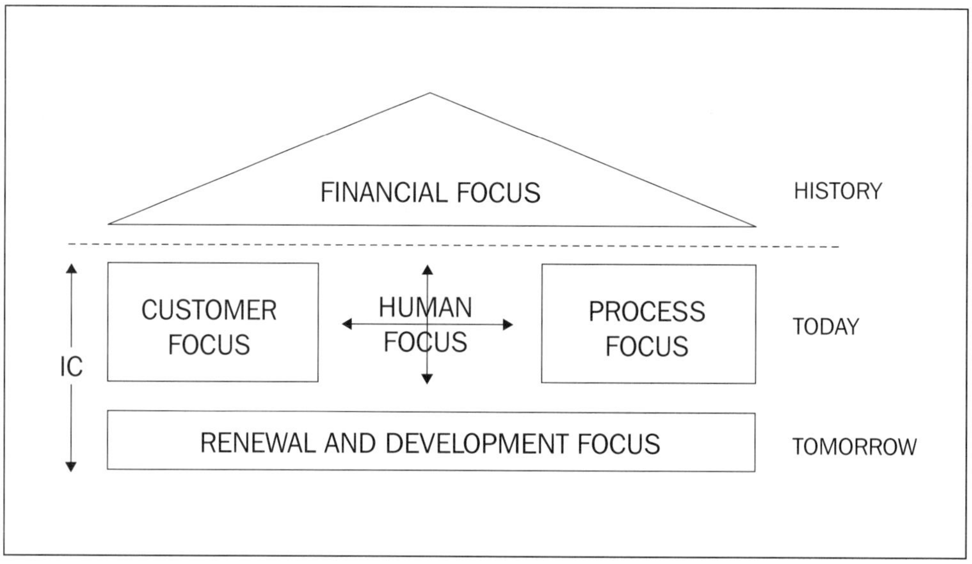

The Balanced Scorecard (Fig. 7.2) fits very well with an Intellectual Capital management strategy as it allows you to look at your organisation from four different aspects. The Balanced Scorecard links performance measures by asking:

- How do we look to our shareholders?

- How do our customers see us?

- What must we excel at?

- Can we continue to improve and create value?

Fig. 7.2 Balanced Scorecard (b)

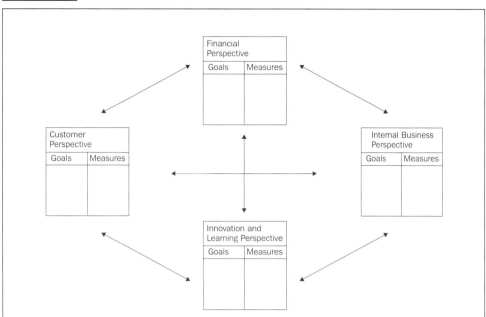

Intellectual Capital Services Ltd (ICS) is an organisation that carries out research and offers consultancy in the management, measurement and valuation of Intellectual Capital. If after reading this book you are interested in pursuing Intellectual Capital management further, ICS may be able to help your business by identifying what your intangible assets are, how they interact and whether they are being best utilised. ICS can also help you create a measurement system around Intellectual Capital value creation. Further information on ICS can be found on their web site at http://www.intcap.com or you can email them directly at intcap@intcap.com.

KEY ISSUES AND BENEFITS

Each chapter of this book has been very much focused on the benefits that can be achieved by adopting an Intellectual Capital management strategy. By organising your company in such a way as to exploit your hidden value you should immediately gain an advantage over your closest competitors.

> Studies have shown that where there are high levels of strategic capability in the HR function, companies tend to have higher levels of financial performance.

In broad terms, the following specific benefits could be reasonably expected to accrue as a result of the successful implementation of an Intellectual Capital management strategy:

- better informed decision making;

- a widespread awareness and adoption of best practice across all functions;

- an improvement in the quality of all that you do;

- a ready supply of skilled and knowledgeable resources;

- more rapid development of solutions and problem resolution;

- the removal of dependence on key individuals;

- increased financial returns from existing resources.

Think and organise differently

Combining varieties of knowledge and experience creates further Intellectual Capital and you should therefore organise your company so that formal and informal interaction can take place to facilitate the sharing of ideas.

Over-organised, traditional working structures tend to separate rather than connect groups. Structures need to be put in place that will encourage creativity and innovation. In the technology age there really is little reason for work teams to sit together. Have you ever considered having random seating arrangements to encourage the cross fertilisation of ideas?

Knowledge sharing is much more likely to take place between people who know and trust each other. Trust between people is normally created through social interaction and you should therefore physically structure your company to encourage socialisation amongst colleagues. Vocational groups or communities of practice do not have to follow standard business organisational structures. Allowing like-minded groups to meet will encourage people to break out of their traditional work patterns.

Company culture

As an organisation AIT has, from the outset, developed a mindset, structure and culture that are essential for the free flow of knowledge within and between teams, individuals, vocations and departments. Together, these elements provide the open and cooperative environment in which knowledge sharing can be facilitated, recognised and rewarded, and in which organisational learning can flourish to the benefit of all AIT's stakeholders.

In your own organisational culture you will need to ensure that there are high levels of trust, openness and teamwork between your employees and between your company and its stakeholders. To encourage creativity you will need to ensure that there is diversity amongst the workforce, that people are open to criticism and that the company has a tolerance of failure. It is essential that all staff and stakeholders feel loyalty towards your company. Loyalty will blossom if people have a strong identification with the company's values.

Knowledge management is not necessarily about capturing what somebody knows but about encouraging people to share their thinking. At the outset the personal benefits of knowledge sharing must be made clear to your staff. Financially rewarding employees for knowledge sharing will foster an environment where people will only share if they are paid to do so. Therefore you should reward knowledge sharing with further knowledge, for example a training course or a book. As your culture changes and the benefits of working together to achieve results becomes self-evident, individuals will adapt their behaviour accordingly.

The pitfalls

Adopting an Intellectual Capital management strategy will take time, will take effort and will invariably require upfront investment. As long as this investment is understood it should not be a barrier to adopting such an approach. However, it is essential that a measurement system is devised to enable the company to show the return on this investment. Beware that an Intellectual Capital management strategy will fail if there is no coherent vision and no clear ownership of that vision.

> The Cranfield School of Management results, reported in *Releasing the Value of Knowledge*, highlight a crucial lack of leadership as the key element in the failure of a knowledge management strategy.

Re-evaluating your Human Capital may help you consolidate your skills base and identify those staff with skills that are no longer of value to the business. If you decide not to retrain those staff, an Intellectual Capital strategy could lead to redundancies which will not be good for overall morale.

An Intellectual Capital measurement policy may expose weaknesses in the fabric of the organisation, even though the balance sheet looks reasonably healthy. Senior management may not wish to expose the frailties in their business potential and the financial numbers may not stand up to closer scrutiny after the reading of the Intellectual Capital report. Those businesses that are happy to display and discuss their Intellectual Capital measurements will raise questions about those businesses that are unwilling to report on their intangibles.

> A recent article by Narayanan, Pinches, Kelm and Lander entitled 'The influence of voluntary disclosed qualitative information' in *Strategic Management Journal* (Vol. 21, No. 7) reported that companies who are able to make meaningful disclosures about their long-term prospects achieved more satisfactory market valuations than those that did not.

To publish, or not to publish your Intellectual Capital results is a decision you will need to give careful consideration to. However, be warned that the Financial Accounting Standards Body is currently looking at how companies should report on areas such as performance measures and forward-looking projections.

APPOINTING A DIRECTOR OF INTELLECTUAL CAPITAL

Whomever you first appoint to develop your Intellectual Capital strategy needs to be a corporate strategist who can set goals and create measures for intangible assets and relate this to business potential. Your Intellectual Capital director needs to understand what the organisation is trying to achieve, and be capable of devising a strategy to help it get there.

The ideal Director of Intellectual Capital will need a mixture of skills that covers organisational behaviour and people development; he or she must have an understanding of how people learn and must have the ability to devise technological solutions to improve human connectivity and corporate efficiency.

8

Intellectual Capital management

INTELLECTUAL CAPITAL – A SUMMARY

Smart, forward-thinking organisations have already identified their Intellectual Capital and are already investing in the intangibles of their company to secure their future. To create an Intellectual Capital management strategy you need to consider each of the components shown in Fig. 8.1 and, more importantly, consider the inter-relations between each of the strands.

Fig. 8.1 Intellectual Capital components

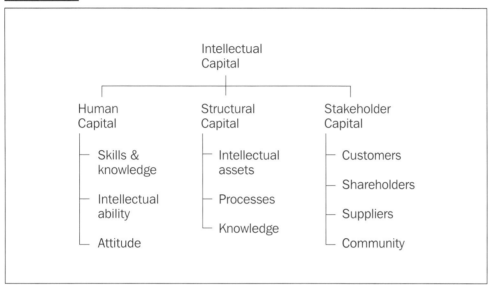

Taking each of the components in turn you should decide on what you will measure and on how those measurements will be collected and analysed. The analysis of these measurements is crucial to help you understand where further investment will be needed.

Effective Intellectual Capital management will make your company sustainable, efficient and profitable and will give you true competitive advantage.

CONCLUSION

The world is changing, perhaps more rapidly than we could ever have imagined twenty years ago. In the industrial age companies were not that worried about what they knew – it was far more important to buy machinery and gain maximum efficiency from that machinery. Nowadays, in the knowledge economy, companies are becoming ever more dependent on their intangible assets. New companies are emerging that do not own anything tangible and yet they are able to obtain financial backing based on their potential for growth. Therefore, we need to find new ways of measuring and monitoring a business.

Intellectual Capital management is concerned with exploiting the potential of all intangible resources, both within and outside of the organisation. An Intellectual Capital strategy will ultimately save time and effort, will ensure better internal and external communication, will give better customer service and will bring products more rapidly to market.

Intellectual Capital is not an isolated initiative but an agreed state of mind. This new mindset has to be pervasive throughout the whole organisation. The Intellectual Capital strategy has to be aligned with the overall business strategy, and it has to have strong leadership in a corporate culture that encourages employees to develop and share knowledge.

Finally, the one-line summation of this book is that an Intellectual Capital management strategy is concerned with extracting value from all of your current resources to improve bottom line performance.

Managing your Intellectual Capital will be costly and time consuming, but ask yourself this question ... can you afford not to do it?